6.16.96

To D[illegible]

Father's Day

Much Love,

RMcL

beachcombing at miramar

beachcombing at miramar

THE QUEST FOR AN AUTHENTIC LIFE

richard bode

A Time Warner Company

Grateful acknowledgment is given to quote from the following:
"Why Do I Love You," written by Jerome Kern and Oscar Hammerstein II. Copyright © 1927 PolyGram International Publishing, Inc. Copyright Renewed. Used by Permission. All Rights Reserved.
"This Dim and Ptolemaic Man," from Selected Poems of John Peale Bishop *by John Peale Bishop. Copyright © 1941 John Peale Bishop; copyright renewed © 1969 Margaret G. H. Bronson. Reprinted with the permission of Scribner, an imprint of Simon & Schuster.*

Warner Books, Inc., 1271 Avenue of the Americas, New York, NY 10020

A Time Warner Company

Printed in the United States of America

First Printing: June 1996

10 9 8 7 6 5 4 3 2 1

Library of Congress Cataloging-in-Publication Data
Bode, Richard.
Beachcombing at Miramar : the quest for an authentic life / Richard Bode.
p. cm.
ISBN 0-446-51867-0
1. Spiritual life. 2. Bode, Richard. 3. Beachcombing—California—Miramar. 4. Miramar (Calif.)—Description and travel. I. Title.
BL624.B588 1996
818'.5403—dc20
[B] *95-42480*
CIP

Book design by Barbara Balch

for julian bach

who believed in me before I believed in myself

contents

It is something to be able to paint a particular picture, or to carve a statue, and so to make a few objects beautiful; but it is far more glorious to carve and paint the very atmosphere and medium through which we look, which morally we can do.

—*HENRY DAVID THOREAU*

beachcombing at miramar

one

the child sees

I've been walking the sands of Miramar for a full year now, and during that time I've met many people who say they would like to become a beachcomber like me. They view it as the easiest job in the world. They think all it takes is the proper garb: white canvas pants rolled up to the knees, faded blue denim shirt, and straw hat to protect their face from the sun. A few actually go to a fancy store and pay a fancy price for garments they believe will change them into the sort of person they think they would like to be.

I see them strolling the shore for a month, a week, a few days, their heads down, plucking stones and shells from the sand. They pause to chat with me, pulling a sea-washed treasure from a deep pocket, as if they had found an amulet they lost a long time ago. But in due course they disappear, having returned, I suppose, to that other occupation they had been so desperate to leave behind.

They seem not to know, when they wander to the edge of the sea, that a beachcomber's life is a demanding one that calls for discipline and zeal. One must venture down to the beach every day without fail and splash ankle-deep in the white surf or walk barefoot on the hot sand. But it's not the hiking; it's the endless seeing that causes the psychic strain. It's the richness of life in the tidal zone, the sea palm and bull kelp, the limpet shells and mole crabs. Someone not used to such abundance can grow weary quickly trying to gather it all in.

In my wanderings on this stretch of beach, I've learned to pace myself so that I'm not overwhelmed. I don't run, I don't walk rapidly, I don't attempt to raise my pulse rate; I'm not here to lose weight or exercise my lungs. I'm here to watch my shadow, sometimes short and sometimes long, depending on the position of the fleeting sun over my head.

I'm not a collector, at least not in the conventional sense of the word. Like my forebears, I'm a hunter-gatherer, but not of objects, although I once brought back to my house above the dunes a worn Monterey pinecone and a smooth piece of driftwood on which someone had carved the words: "Life is but a dream." I tacked the sculpted plaque to my front door where I confront those fateful words each time I come home.

Nor am I a painter, although I wish I were, but I'm searching for those unexpected images that arise from nowhere to define the nature of my life and remind me who I am. My father was a painter, a real painter who worked in oils. When I was a boy, no more than six, he showed me how to draw human figures with ovals for head, torso, legs, and arms. But he died before the next lesson, and so I never progressed; I draw as a man exactly as I did as a boy.

But the hunger lingers in me, so I must content myself with what I can do. Long ago I gave up the idea of putting pigment on canvas and began to paint the day itself, the air I breathe, which I discovered I could do. I can take the life that swirls about me, bend and distort it to give it perspective, place it in a mental frame and carry it with me wherever I go. I can't say if it's easier or harder than drawing on a sketch pad, but I have no choice; I'm driven to this place, this habitat, this beach at Miramar, as surely as if I were a tern or a gull.

I have come to gather scenes—quiet scenes, turbulent scenes—that remain etched forever in my memory. In my own small way I am waiting for what I love, waiting for love itself, watching carefully, awake to every possibility, for I have no idea what will appear when I least expect it.

Here, at my feet, foam from the surf collects

with the seaweed and blows across the beach in the gentle breeze like a serpent's beard. I gather the fluff in the cup of my hand and gaze into a globule of air, reflecting a world within a world. I burst the bubble with my finger, and the world I saw a moment ago explodes. But I behold it still in my mind's eye, a vivid image of what once was, and so it's as real to me now as it was before.

Where the dunes part, a couple emerges, pushing a three-wheeled buggy that holds a child. They pause in the middle of the beach to do their warm-ups, bending knees, stretching hamstrings. When ready, they push the buggy onto the wet, compacted sand and jog toward me. Heads down, eyes forward, they gain speed. They are serious runners; glancing neither to left nor right, they run in unison: left leg, right leg, left leg, right. A raven rises over the dunes; a sea lion surfaces in the breakers. They are unaware. But the child in the buggy swings his head back and forth from land to sea, from sea to land. The child sees.

two

dollars in the sand

There are two ways to beachcomb, and both appeal to me. One is to scan the horizon, gazing over the breakers or down the misty shore until indistinct shapes reveal themselves for what they are. The other is to stroll head down, searching for treasures buried in the sun-bleached sand. I never know which impulse—to scan or to search—will sway me until I wander down to the edge of the sea.

This morning I find myself in a searching mood, so I amble aimlessly, tending southward, gazing intently at the circle of sand about my feet. I'm not sure how decisions as subtle as these are made, or if they're made at all. Like a migrating bird, I move by instinct, my behavior governed by forces beyond myself: the brightness of the sun, the angle of the wind, the running of the tide. The elements mix their magic in my mind and my legs respond.

The outgoing tide has exposed a broad swath of wet sand. The sanderlings are here, feeding on the flats, their needle bills probing for tiny mollusks and burrowing worms. Their legs are barely as long as my longest finger, yet they strut at twice my speed. Were I to move at their pace, I would be miles down the shore by now.

The roaring breakers chase them up the beach; they chase the retreating surf down the beach. I marvel at how precisely attuned they are to play their tireless game of tag with the surging sea. They seem to know intuitively how fast a wave will wash across the sand. They run just rapidly enough to keep ahead of the foaming water as it rushes in—and follow it as it rolls back out.

I feel a kinship with these birds, as if we are bound by a common purpose, despite the outward differences in the way we behave. Their pace appears so frantic; mine so leisurely. They're probing for food; I'm searching for the bounty washed in by the waves. Who is to say that my quest is less crucial than theirs, or theirs more vital than mine?

When I arrived at Miramar, I wasn't nearly as rich as I am today. All I had was my van, my clothes, my typewriter, my record player, my unabridged dictionary, and a few favorite books. After years of accumulation, I had an irresistible urge to simplify, to pare my possessions down to bare essentials, to tread as lightly, as freely as possible over the face of the land.

I also had a check, which, if converted to cash, might have filled a shoe box with twenty-dollar bills. That was a residue, my fractional share of the substantial store of assets I had divided with my wife of thirty years under the terms of our divorce. I had earned the money, but I didn't need it. She hadn't earned the money, but she did need it. From those contrary stances, approaches to life as much as bargaining positions, we forged an agreement. She acquired financial security; I purchased my freedom, which was more precious to me than breath itself.

My friends and counselors were dismayed. "Don't be so hasty!" they said. "The day will come when you'll wish you had the money you gave to her."

They meant well, as friends so often do, but I felt then, and I'm certain now, that their advice was founded on the mistaken assumption that money is a solid, which, once relinquished, can never be regained. But money isn't a solid; it's a fluid, like water. The cupful I spill over one side of the ship, I scoop up again on the other side.

I left my marriage exactly as I entered it three decades earlier. I had no mortgage, no credit-card balances, no bank loans. What I did have, somewhere in the middle of my mind, was a gyroscope, pointing me in a direction, telling me where I had to go. I set out, driving through snow-covered cornfields and prairie, crossing the Continental Divide, going from one coast to the other in quest of a place that felt like home.

And now I am here, walking the beach, watching the fist-sized shorebirds as they feed. They have no cache, no hoard, no store; like me, they live by their wits, taking what they want from the sea.

How is it, I ask myself, that I have so little money, yet I live so well?

I know the answer even before the question has filtered through my brain. It lies, in part, in what I have shed, the material encumbrances of life that once weighed me down, and, in part, in the useful objects I discover—the bric-a-brac, the artifacts, the relics, the castaway bits and pieces of civilization—as I comb the sand. A glass bottle with a narrow neck serves as a vase, and a stiff canvas sail—a remnant from a schooner dashed against the offshore rocks—makes an awing over my sunbaked deck.

What mystifies me most is the way the sea anticipates my needs. Once I stumbled upon a teak chest that some wealthy yachtsman probably ripped from his cabin and tossed overboard as he sailed by. I don't believe he intended it for me, but the sea, in its infinite wisdom, knew my stereo was sitting on the floor. I dragged it to my beach house, washed it off, dried it out, and now it anchors a corner of my living room. My turntable rests on top, my records on the sturdy shelves below, and every morning at breakfast I have a concerto with my scrambled eggs.

A vast kelp bed lies a hundred yards off the beach; the sea grass breaks loose and collects in clumps along the shore. Sand fleas hop about the tangled mass, which I skirt for fear these scavengers will leap into my rolled-up pants and feast on me. I veer closer to the water's edge; the surf splashes over my legs as high as my thighs, and as it draws away, I see a chalk white disk in the sand.

It's a sand dollar. I lay it flat in my palm and study its distinctive engraving: five petals, which remind me that this isn't a living creature, but a skeleton. The petals are fossil imprints of its breathing tubes. But the flower is so exquisitely etched on its convex surface that it might be the lithotint of a master artist, a symphony on stone.

I uncover a second and third, gleaming in the sand, each smaller than the one before. In descending order, they seem to me like a fifty-cent piece and a quarter—although my local bank places no value on them in its current rate of exchange. I spread all three across my open hand and study them one at a time. On the smallest I detect traces of lavender-gray spines that flowed in the ocean current like a field of grass in the wind when it was still alive.

My toes are numb from the cold water, so I move up the beach to dry them in the warm sand. The upper shore is littered with beach drift and tide wrack, splintered logs washed down from the redwood forests, broken stalks of seaweed and the brittle, whitened bones of birds. I pause to inspect a piece of cork, and as I do, I see four soaked dollar bills lying by my feet. There's no doubt about their denomination, for I can plainly make out the dour face of George Washington staring up at me. I pick them up, rub them between my fingers, hold them up to the noonday sun. In the upper-left-hand corner I read the words: THIS NOTE IS LEGAL TENDER FOR ALL DEBTS, PUBLIC AND PRIVATE.

I look up and down the beach, deserted both ways. Maybe the money belongs to a surfer, but there's no sign of a human head bobbing in the waves. I have a choice. I can leave the bills on the beach, knowing the tide will claim them before their rightful owner passes this way again, or I can pocket them—and that's what I decide to do. I have the feeling these saturated notes are no different from the bottle, the canvas sail, the teak chest, or any of the other gifts that drift in from the sea.

I climb the sloping beach and flop back against a dune. I close my eyes and try to decipher the coincidence of these different kinds of dollars in such proximity along the shore. When I look for sand dollars, I discover real dollars; when I look for real dollars, I never find them, and I go by the sand dollars without ever knowing that they're there. Suddenly I realize something about myself I didn't know before. All my life I've been tending toward this common meeting ground of the sacred and the profane, the savage and the divine.

I might have been a millionaire; I mean that literally. Ages ago, long before I came to Miramar, I was employed by a New York public-relations agency, which has since grown to one of the largest in the world. That firm had a highly seductive profit-sharing plan, one calculated to keep its workers from taking flight, and I was part of it.

Each year the firm set aside a percentage of my salary in my name. If I remained in the plan for ten years, I would be fully vested; that is, all the monies set aside in my name would actually belong to me. If I quit the company after ten years, I would be comfortable. If

I quit after twenty years, I would be rich. If I quit after thirty years, I would have gathered unto myself sufficient wealth to care for myself, my children, and my children's children for generations to come.

When I joined the firm, the financial vice president told me this was the way I could build an estate. He didn't ask me if I wanted to build an estate. He assumed I did, and at that early juncture of my life I assumed I did, too. But the cubicle they assigned me had sealed windows and the duct over my laminated desk emitted fetid air. I had to sign in every morning and sign out every night.

Every day promptly at noon I would leave the office and spend my lunch hour wandering the city streets, taking in the sights and sounds. Some days I would stroll through United Nations Plaza, lean against the railing above the East River, and watch the boats cruise by. Other days I would stroll to Rockefeller Center, sit in a pew in St. Thomas Church, or visit the Central Park menagerie.

After a while I began to stretch my one-hour jaunts to two. I would walk to the ferry slip at the Battery, or up Riverside Drive, near the Hudson, as far as the Soldiers' and Sailors' Memorial, or across town to the turmoil at Times Square. I didn't know it at the time, but I was beachcombing on Forty-second Street,

Columbus Circle, and the Avenue of the Americas, preparing myself for my true profession.

My boss said nothing, for I was a good worker and I made up for these extended lunch hours in other ways. One year I won an award of one thousand dollars for the most creative project in the agency. But I derived no satisfaction from it because I saw no value in what I had done. The real dollars were present, but the sand dollars were absent, and, to me, the one without the other was like a wedding without a bride.

I left after six years, forsaking the money in the profit-sharing trust. Some of the people I worked with a quarter of a century ago are there still. That is one of life's mysteries. Why is it that some will stay and some will go? I bumped into one of my former colleagues in a SoHo bistro shortly before I left for Miramar, and he remembered my departure very well.

"I always saw that as an act of tremendous courage," he said.

I believe he meant it, too. But he was wrong, although I didn't tell him so. I can no more say I acted with courage when I quit that job than I can say a man who is suffocating acts with courage when he tries to breathe.

I didn't go directly to Miramar. I had other places to go, other lives to lead. I had mortgage payments to meet and a wife and four lively children to feed. I became a self-employed freelance writer, producing articles for magazines and speeches for corporate executives. I wasn't paid by the hours I put in, but by the work I produced. When a paycheck came in the mail, I knew exactly what it was for. I could hold the manuscript in my hand; I could read my words on the printed page.

My work took me into a world that might otherwise have been closed to me, and I discovered how it worked. I went to Indiana to see the flaming hearth of a steel plant, and to Vermont to see airborne computer chips floating down an automated production line. I went to a field campus in the Sierra to interview a noted economist about the underlying causes of inflation, and to Washington, D.C., to ask experts to explain the reasons for the nation's lagging industrial productivity. I met with the chairman of a blue-chip corporation on the top floor of a Wall Street skyscraper, and with a conveyor-belt operator at the bottom of a sandpit.

I went to all those places and I did all those things, and I don't regret a moment, for each experience contributed mightily to the sum of who I am and what I know. But the day came when my children were no longer children and had moved into lives of their own, and I knew the hour had also come for me to move on to a place in life I had never been before.

And now I stand with waves at my feet and words spoken on a hillside two thousand years ago blowing like spindrift through my brain.

"Consider the lilies of the field, how they grow . . ."

How they grow! There's the nub—that phrase tucked in so innocently, which we so easily overlook. I wonder how stunted I would be today if I were so worried about what I would eat, or what I would drink, or what I would wear that I never dared venture to Miramar.

I stoop to pick up a pale flight feather, and as I do, a puff catches the blade and blows it away. I chase it down, holding it by the hollow quill, rolling it between my thumb and index finger, a wand so slight, so delicate, I hardly know it's there. I judge by its length and color that it once belonged to a western gull who had no further need of it, so he left it on the beach for me to find and use in whatever way I choose. I could make a pen of it, but I know there's nothing I can do with it that will give it greater utility than it has already served in the plumage of the bird. I decide to take it home and place it on my desk as a constant reminder of the weightless strength it takes to fly.

Below the low-tide line, I see a pink scallop in the dark sand, exposed by a retreating wave. I pluck it out and examine it carefully. It's a near-perfect shell, one with a small chip in its margin, which is how I know it's what I'm looking for. I drop it into my shirt pocket. Later I will add it to the collection of periwinkles, razor clams, whelks, and mussels that decorate my kitchen windowsill. I display only those with minor flaws; it's the blemish that gives a shell its character.

I find a keyhole limpet and a turban snail. I put them to my nose and breathe in, hoping to catch the scent of tidal pools, but they are salt-washed and sandblasted, as sweet smelling as line-dried clothes. It occurs to me that I could string my shells together into a wampum necklace and offer it as legal tender to purchase this strip of land, this stretch of beach, this Miramar! And then I realize that it isn't necessary for me to barter for what I want, because, by the immutable laws of nature, it is already mine.

three

a lonely *stretch* of beach

The splintery deck of my beach house runs clear across the front, facing the declining sun. In the late afternoon I gather myself there with my make-believe watercolors and the easel of my mind. I'm a patient man; I can sit for hours if I must, motionless as a heron, waiting for a proper image to appear. I feel as if something momentous is about to happen and I want to witness it when it does. It may be huge, like a rogue wave washing over the dunes, or small, like a hermit crab crawling out of the sea.

I wasn't always filled with this sense of expectancy, as if at any moment the universe was going to reveal its deepest and darkest secrets to me. When I arrived at Miramar, I was like a castaway on a desert island, alone and suspicious of every living thing. But I feel now as I imagine Paul Gauguin must have felt when at long last he reached Tahiti, the land of his waking dreams.

"I began to work—notes, sketches of all sorts," he wrote in his memoir. "Everything in the landscape blinded and dazzled me." As he painted, he shed the leathery skin of civilization and became the naked savage—"my body bare, except for the essential part"—he was meant to be.

Immersing himself in *noa noa*, the heady fragrance of Oceania, he met Tehamana, his lover, ". . . and bliss followed upon bliss. Each day at dawn," he wrote, "the light in my home was radiant. The gold of Tehamana's face bathed everything around it, and both of us went naturally and simply, as in paradise, to a nearby stream to refresh ourselves."

Tehamana, Tehamana—I say it over and over, as if I could wring the mystery from it by repeating it softly under my breath. How far, I wonder, must a man journey to find a woman with such a name?

I feel as if I understand the painter's impulse better now than ever before, for these long, quiet days have taught me that I am less alone on this stretch of beach than I was on the streets of New York. Gauguin wasn't drawn to isolation; he was fleeing from it. It was loneliness that drove him to the South Seas, the searing loneliness that overwhelms us in a faceless crowd or a loveless marriage, the loneliness that evaporates in the gentle warmth of a tropical breeze. The gravitational pull of that faraway place was so powerful that he had no choice except to forsake his wife, his children, and his job, and migrate, as a swallow migrates when the season turns.

What he wanted to do, what he had to do, was paint with a moral intensity. He had to paint—not paint his canvases, which are masterworks in themselves, but paint himself, paint the very medium through which he looked, which is the more enormous task by far. He had to create the man he wanted to be, and he could accomplish that miracle, which we call transfiguration, only on a soil that was congenial to his heart and soul.

I believe we are all bent upon this course, whether we know it or not, because, like Everyman, we are all caught up in the same morality play. I see now it is so for me, and I understand how it came to pass that in the aftermath of my marriage I made my solitary journey to the sands of Miramar. I was alone when I arrived, more alone than I had ever been before. But day by day, as I dwelled with my aloneness, my loneliness faded, and my life as the sole creator of myself began.

I covet my solitude and I try to protect it, to defend myself against the intrusions, the interruptions, the well-intentioned invitations of others who want to drag me into their way of life, which is the only life they know. I resist their efforts as best I can, but each time the phone rings I'm afraid it's the couple across the road, who can't bear to see me sitting by myself on my deck, staring at the sea.

They have made it clear to me that they think I'm lonely because I'm alone, so they ask me to dinner at least once a week because they are sure I could use, as they put it, "some cheering up—some company." But when I join them, I find they are the dispirited ones and that the onus is on me. I feel as if I'm not so much their guest as their entertainment for the night. They want me to be charming, my conversation witty, skimming the surface, never delving too deep or disclosing too much, and that is more of a burden than I can bear.

I would share my inner life with them if they would let me, but I know if I revealed the intimate details of my days, they would be embarrassed, as if I had undressed in front of them and stood stark naked in their living room. I try to talk to them one at a time as individuals, as man and woman instead of husband and wife. But they make it impossible to talk to one without talking to both, and they are in constant contention as they try to convey what they think and how they feel.

"What we believe . . ." the wife will say, and the husband will modify her statement, explaining what she meant to say, and she will take exception to his interruption, claiming he misinterpreted what she said. He will smile wanly, conceding her point, and she will acknowledge his apology with a nod and go on talking about their joint point of view, as if they were some mythological beast with two bodies and one head.

Whenever they vie with each other in this way in my presence, I have no choice but to sit there quietly, sipping my soup, hoping against all hope that they will find a common ground before dessert. It's all I can do to keep from blurting out that he doesn't have to speak for her and she doesn't have to speak for him—that he can have his perceptions and she can have hers and the two don't have to jibe. But that simple thought never seems to occur to them, so they go on playing out their life-and-death struggle in a minor key, never realizing how portentous it is.

As the evening draws to a close, I am filled with sadness—for I sense the hopelessness of their plight and I know there is nothing I can do. I see how they are trapped in their loneliness, and how each blames the other for the isolation they can't escape. Since they have never learned how to be by themselves, they have never learned how to be together. It seems to me as though they skirmish because they have nothing better to do; the combat itself is a form of relief, a way of letting them know they are still alive.

But this evening I don't have to cope with the couple across the road. The interval before the sun sinks below the horizon belongs to me and me alone. I rise from my deck chair and head for the kitchen. I shell some peas, stuff them into my pocket, and wander barefoot—nibbling as I go—to the sacred place where the surf meets the land.

I arrive as the rim of the sun touches the edge of the sea. The light glints off the water and strikes a polished object beside my little toe. I squat and pick it up; it's an oval piece of pale blue beach glass worn smooth by the waves. I stare into its clear surface, as if there's a scene hidden somewhere within its reflective planes—and then I remember seeing a long time ago another piece of beach glass like the one in my hand.

It was at a dinner party given by friends—the husband, a carpenter; the wife, a schoolteacher—to celebrate their tenth anniversary. During dessert, the husband reached into his pocket and took out a small white box, which he held in his calloused hand. Silently, he offered the gift to his wife, his eyes wide with anticipation. The room grew quiet as the guests witnessed the carpenter's simple gesture, more eloquent than words.

I knew that the box contained a triangular piece of glass set in a brooch, for the husband had showed it to me beforehand. He told me that he and his wife had found it on their wedding trip while strolling together along a beach beside the Irish Sea. They had handed it back and forth, admiring its rare beauty, sure that it was an artifact from the Roman Conquest and that it had washed ashore at that moment in that place just for them.

The carpenter had pocketed the glass, taken it home, and kept it in his dresser drawer, planning to give it to his wife on their tenth anniversary. He had never mentioned it to her, but he had never forgotten, and now the day had come, the time had arrived, and he was sitting at their dinner table with friends, holding a white box in the palm of his hand.

His wife glanced at the extended hand, but she didn't take the gift; instead, she pointed at the leather brace around his swollen wrist, which he had sprained while making new cabinets for their kitchen. Turning to her guests, she said, "Isn't it amazing how he always manages to hurt himself when he is working around our house?" She tried to pass it off as a lighthearted remark, a gentle tease, but her lips were thin and there was an undercurrent of derision in her voice.

The carpenter had a wonderful face, a lively

face, but his head drooped and his eyes turned sad. He looked at his wife as if she had shot an arrow through his heart. He twisted slowly in his chair and put the white box on a windowsill behind him, out of reach, and asked her to apologize. He smiled when he asked her, but it was clear to me, clear to everyone in the room, that he was wounded by her ridicule.

"Why must I apologize?" she said. "Must I apologize to get the present? Is that the price?"

She was cool, she was logical, she was civilized, and she left her husband with no choice. He was still smiling when he turned, picked up the box, and offered it to her once more. This time she accepted it, opened it, made a fuss over it, passed it around for her guests to see.

"Isn't it beautiful?" she said. But she gave no sign that she remembered where it came from or what it was.

When I think back on that terrible moment, what haunts me most is the face of the carpenter, the glazed smile that masked his anguish and despair. It was as if he was forced to admit to himself for the first time the gap between them, a gap that he could never bridge no matter how hard he tried. I know all too well his sense of futility, for I have been there myself in my own life, and I know how hopelessness seeps into the bones day by dreary day, like some dread disease we know is there but are too scared to recognize. And then one evening we offer a gift, which is the gift of ourselves, and the gift is spurned. But the truth, the inescapable truth, is revealed, and for a while it dazzles us and makes us blind.

I look again at the beach glass in my hand, wondering whether to keep it or throw it away. I decide to pocket it, to save mine as my friend, the carpenter, saved his, because it's too precious a gift to give back to the sea.

I climb higher up the beach to a dune and lie against it. The sun is down but the sand is warm, and I burrow into it up to my knees. The evening star hangs like a lantern in the western sky, so low on the horizon, it looks as if it's stuck atop the mast of a passing ship. A full moon rises against Aquarius, the water bearer, and casts a river of light across the ocean.

I think of the ancients sitting on the beach like me, studying the heavens night after night, painting pictures in the sky: Sagittarius, the archer; Andromeda, the chained lady; Pegasus, the winged horse; Capricornus, the horned goat, and Orion, the mighty hunter with a red star for a shoulder and three bright ones for a belt. What were they dreaming, these early artists, when they sketched their mythic figures on the blackboard of the sky?

The celestial bodies are foreign to me, but I have become more adept at deciphering their signs since I arrived at Miramar. I look for Gemini, my own particular place in the zodiac. The inseparable twins, Castor and Pollux, are out there somewhere on this starry, starry night, and I know that if I wait long enough they will wheel into view. I am drawn to them whenever I find them drifting in unison over my head, flickering symbols of perfect companionship and eternal love.

Is it possible, I wonder, for two people to share the same small piece of sky? Is it possible for me to find a woman who sees the world through my eyes, as I see it through hers? The art of the ancient mythographers tells me this isn't my dream alone, that the desire for union goes far back in human history, dwells deep in the human soul.

Yes, I am alone, and at this moment of my life, that is where I choose to be. Although it may not be the ideal state, I'm consoled by the knowledge that I'm nowhere near as lonely as the mismated husbands and wives I see everywhere. Two individuals who are together but not together, who don't respond to the world about them in the same way, are by far the loneliest people of all. The sun rises and the sun sets; for one it's an incalculable mystery, for the other a time of day.

I burrow deeper into the sand and scan the heavens once more. After a while I close my eyes. When I awake, the air is chill and the morning star is climbing over the dunes.

four

the real world

My phone rings at six in the morning, waking me from a sound sleep. I roll over, pick up the receiver, and before I can say hello, Leo starts to talk. A former colleague, he has been a reliable friend and steady source of work throughout my freelance life. Even so, I want to protest—to tell him that just because it's nine o'clock on his coast doesn't mean it's nine on mine. But I know the futility of that. Leo doesn't recognize time zones or any other conventions, social or natural, that come between him and what he wants.

He begins, as he always does, by praising me. He tells me he has an assignment, something special, which only I can write, he says, "because you're the best." It's a speech for the chief executive of a major corporation to deliver before an august body of businessmen in Geneva, Switzerland. I know what's coming and I try to stop him before he goes too far, but he's an express train roaring down the track. He dangles a substantial fee, one that might have proven irresistible at some other moment in my life, and then he adds, "This speech will be easy, extremely easy, especially for you. The guy knows exactly what he wants to say. All he needs are the words."

"Leo—" I begin, but that's as far as I get.

"I know, I know," he says. "You've taken a solemn vow never to write another speech as long as you live. But this one is different. This one is easy, and you have to admit the money is good—very good. Besides, I need you. I need you for this assignment and I won't let you turn me down."

"Leo—" I say, not trying to hide my exasperation, but he interrupts me again.

"Look," he says, "don't say anything. Don't say anything now. Think it over. Take twenty-four hours. I'll call you tomorrow, same time, and then we can make arrangements to put you on a plane and bring you back to the real world."

The receiver clicks.

I pull on some clothes and head for the beach. The morning mist is in, filling the air with a fine drizzle that coats my skin and soaks my hair. I can hear the raucous call of a gull somewhere beyond the breakers and the cutting blare of the foghorn, like clockwork, every ten seconds, pulling me toward the head of the harbor. I go the back way, along the beach, over the breakwater, and when I reach the restaurant on the pier, I settle into a booth by a window and watch the sky, growing lighter by the minute as the sun burns the fog away.

The waitress knows my order without asking, for she has, by her own word, served me "a thousand times." She brings me a large glass of fresh-squeezed orange juice, waffles, and a cup of hot water with a wedge of lemon. As I raise the cup to my lips, I realize that my hand is trembling, as if my entire being were under assault. I can see Leo clearly, lean and electric, pacing around his huge mahogany desk, and I can hear his insistent voice echoing in my brain, urging me to return to the real world.

I feel my anger rising. It's infuriating—this blind presumption of his that he knows what's real and I don't. I feel his presence—he is sitting across the table from me and I hear myself saying to his face what I failed to say on the phone.

The real world, the real world, where is it, Leo, and what does it look like? Is it up in the mountain or down in the valley or across the sea? Is it urban or rural, a place of commerce or a place of art? Does it exist in the executive suite or on the factory floor? Will I find it under the rain-forest canopy or in a grocery store? Please tell me where I can find the real world, Leo, its longitude, its latitude, for I long to go there, settle there, make it my home.

And what of this would-be speechmaker who knows exactly what he wants to say but lacks the words? What about him, Leo? Does he dwell in the real world or is he deluding himself? If his world is real, how is it that he's so speechless? He's a speechless man eager to make a speech, but before he mounts the dais, puts on his glasses, and clears his throat, he must hire a ghost to supply his words.

And who is that ghost, Leo? That ghost is me. I am the ghost who turns out words at a unit price—like so many parts rolling off an assembly line. I string those words together, and when I'm finished, the would-be speechmaker has my words, my thoughts, my sentiments, and so, whether he admits it or not, he has reduced himself to a ghost, too.

In the real world, Leo, I would be giving the speech and he would be sitting in the audience, listening. Or he would have written his own speech and I would be sitting in the audience, listening. Or, if he had no words of his own, he would remain in his office, running his company, and I would remain in my beach house, sorting shells.

But that's not what happens, Leo. What happens is that speechwriter and speechmaker cross over into each other's domain, they invade each other's souls, and once they commit that trespass, they cease being themselves. They become apparitions, phantoms, mere shades of who they are.

Where is the reality of that, Leo?

The words pour like the waters of a swollen river racing downstream after a thaw. I lean back in my seat, considerably relieved, even though I have delivered an imaginary monologue to someone who isn't there.

Will Leo understand? Will he ever understand? I have to ask myself that question, but as soon as I ask it, I know the question is wrong. No, Leo will not understand. I could go on forever trying to explain how I feel, but he will not understand. I realize that now, and in the knowing, I find the tension melting away. The one question, the only question that matters, is whether I must go on asking the question.

It's not my mission in life, I tell myself, to make Leo understand.

I pay my bill and wander into the sunlight, following a path between a steep rise of land and the sea. I pause beside a rocky ledge and glance over the waves. The tide is coming in and the swells are huge. I imagine them rising from canyon depths somewhere beyond the horizon and rolling endlessly, as they have been rolling for aeons, until they spend their pent-up energy crashing against the shore.

The beach is isolated, but I'm not alone. A purple shore crab is here, skittering sideways, disappearing into a crevice, and the outcroppings are covered with limpets and barnacles. In the intertidal zone, imbedded in the mud, I see a congregation of sea anemones clustered together, forming a soggy mat. I touch one tentatively, tenderly, and it contracts its oval disk, flooding itself with water as it does. I kneel and dig around it with my hands, intending to lift it out, but it's firmly rooted, and it keeps withdrawing, pulling away from my touch, growing smaller and sinking deeper in the sand.

I am calm now, much calmer than before. I am under the influence of the sea and the abundant life that emerges from the sea, species evolving from species, each questing for its natural home.

I think of my early ancestors following the moist edge of the glacier, learning to build fires, learning to sew, learning to cultivate the land. How is it that some became hunters, some gatherers, some fishers, some planters of seeds? Was this simple adaptation? Did some become farmers because the soil was there, or were they farmers from birth, searching for fertile soil to till? Did man shape the land, or did the land from which he sprang shape him? I suspect the latter is so, although I can offer no proof beyond what I sense in these reflective moments when I wander beside the sea.

I feel as though I am an animal with a homing instinct, tending toward the one place on earth that is native to me. I have spent a lifetime moving toward a specific place—a place called Miramar. The journey has been long and arduous, but it is a journey that I had to undertake, for I know now that as long as I remained in a place that was wrong for me, I was not in the real world.

I pass a salt pond where a marsh hawk dips and soars close to the cattails, searching for prey. A black phoebe flits from a bush and feeds on the wing, seizing invisible insects from the air. A snowy egret wades in the shoals, spearing fish, and a belted kingfisher hovers above the placid surface before he plunges and momentarily disappears. Far beyond the breakers a cormorant flies swiftly by, drawing a black thread across the sky.

The birds live near one another; sometimes they mingle—like the quick-footed willets, plovers, and godwits probing the sand. But they never try to imitate or influence one another; each feeds, flies, and nests in its own distinctive way. And the wonder of it is that they all thrive.

It occurs to me that perhaps the human race is like the birds—not a single species, but an order of species, each dwelling in its own habitat. Some of us nest in skyscrapers, some in farmhouses, some in igloos or grass huts, some in riverboats, and some in cottages beside the sea. I have my habitat and Leo has his, and the trouble between us occurs when one or the other of us forgets that we aren't the same kind of bird.

Farther up the beach, I see a woman and a boy hanging on to a dog by its collar. As I get closer, I can see it's a black Labrador. Below them a man is standing knee-deep in the water, frantically waving his arms at the surf. He's shouting, "Here doggy, doggy! Here doggy, doggy! Come here!"

He turns, pointing into the surf, and bellows at a man standing high on the dunes, "Is that your dog?"

The man doesn't respond.

As I approach, he turns to me.

"Is that your dog?" he yells.

A sleek black head bobs up in the breakers, looks at us, and disappears below the surface again.

"If we don't get him out of there," the man shouts, "he's going to drown!"

"That's not a dog," I say.

The man stares at me.

"Of course it's a dog."

"No," I say, "it's a sea lion. And you can call him all you want to, but he's not coming ashore."

five

girl with a crab

I sleep long and late, and when I awake, the sun is halfway up the sky. I step onto my deck and stretch, and as I do, I feel the ease of my life sifting through my bones. The ocean is calm today, as calm as the Pacific can be. There is only a faint offshore breeze, as if sea and land have entered into a temporary truce.

I take to the water's edge, intending to walk, but my body has a will of its own and it wants to run. After a mile I feel beads of sweat collecting on my brow. I want to stop, but my body won't let me—it revels in its surging freedom, and it wants to keep on going toward that ever-receding point where the sea merges with the shore. My legs tire before my breath gives out. When I reach a public beach, I slow down.

The children are there, playing in the sand, splashing in the water, immune to the cold. I stop to watch them, amused by the abandon that comes to them so naturally. Suddenly a small girl bolts from her playmates and races up to me, chattering away.

She is no more than six or seven, and she is carrying a pail filled with seawater. She holds it up so I can see inside. She is exuberant as only a child can be, and she can barely contain herself as she tells her tale to me, a stranger on the beach.

"I found a crab," she says, "and the crab is mine. He'll always be my crab until he dies. When he dies, I'll find another crab, and he'll be mine, too, until he dies."

I kneel on the sand beside her and watch the crab as he tries to claw his way out of the pail.

"He's beautiful," I say. "But maybe he misses his home on the ocean floor."

"Oh no," she says, "he belongs to me! He's my crab and he'll always be my crab!"

She grabs the pail and races down the beach. I watch her. She sets the pail on the sand and joins her friends, who are dashing in and out of the surf.

I continue on my way, walking slowly. After a while I settle on the sand, leaning against a log that has washed in from the sea. I began my jaunt in a joyful mood, but now a disquieting memory, long repressed, rises from my childhood.

I remember playing on a sandy beach when I was a boy, no older than the girl with the crab. I was with my parents and a few of their friends when suddenly one of the men decided to hold me down on my back. He kept me in that position easily, with one hand placed firmly on my chest while I tried in vain to wriggle away. I remember he was laughing, and so were the other adults, as if it were funny, and it wasn't until I burst out in tears, screaming, that he finally let me up. Now, a half century later, I still recall the incident and the way that man restrained me, as if he had a perfect right.

On another occasion, I remember my parents putting me in the backseat of the family car, saying we were going to my grandparents' house. I believed them, for we had made that trip together many times. On the way they stopped in front of a gray building and led me inside, where I was summarily snatched away by a nurse and stuck in a crib with high bars. I had no warning, no idea why I was there, and I stood in the crib, kicking and crying, desperate to escape. Eventually an orderly came, strapped me on a gurney, and wheeled me to an operating room to have my tonsils removed.

I have never quite forgiven my mother or my father for that deception, even though both are long dead. They made a decision to take the easy way out, the way that was easy for them. But would they have behaved in that insensitive way if they saw me, not as a child over whom they had absolute power, but as a person—a thinking, feeling individual who had the same qualms, the same anxieties, the same need for reassurance as they?

I wonder now, as I sit here on this beach, if that is why the girl with the crab affected me so. Of all the evils perpetrated by man, the one that frightens me most is the possibility of being trapped, of being snatched off the street, of being kidnapped, taken hostage, and held against my will. What deed is more cowardly than capturing living beings through cunning or brute strength and confining them in a hostile place for years, perhaps for life?

I saw a snow leopard in a zoo once, and I shall never forget the sight. The curators of the exhibit had created an environment that came as close as possible to the leopard's rocky lair in the Himalayas. They had built a circular cage, perhaps a hundred feet across, and piled boulders against the iron bars to form a lookout and a den.

They had attached a placard to the bars that described the leopard's way of life on a high range halfway around the world. Spectators gathered around and stared at the animal, at his milky coat, his pale spots, his huge paws, and then moved on. But I stayed long after they left, watching the leopard pacing, endlessly pacing, inside his cage.

The thought occurred to me that I owed a debt to those who had gone to so much trouble to display the snow leopard so that curious people like me might see what he looks like and how he behaves. But as I stood there I felt only the presumption of my fellow-man, who had taken this animal from where he evolved, where he was meant to be, and imprisoned him in a city zoo.

The deplorable consequence is that when I go to the zoo, I don't see a snow leopard at all. I don't see his elegance, his stealth, his subtle strength as he moves for miles across the glacial snows of his mountain home. What I see is a displaced creature destined to live out his life in an alien world.

This is a condition of life, one we can't deny no matter how we try to persuade ourselves that the truth is otherwise. There is no choice, no middle ground, no compromise. Once we possess another creature, we alter forever the inherent nature of that creature.

I look over the breakers to the place where the horizon falls away. Do I have dominion over the waves *and over the fish of the sea*? I look over my head at the soaring gulls. Do I have dominion over the sky *and over the fowl of the air*? All my life, all my experience tells me I am not in control—that any attempt on my part to exercise control over every living thing is a sacrilege and doomed to fail.

As children we think we own a crab. As adults we think we own our husbands, our wives, our sons, our daughters. But the only life we own, truly own, is our own.

When my children were first learning to walk, I remember picking them up and holding them close because that is what I had an irresistible impulse to do. Sometimes they wanted the comfort that closeness provides. But usually they quickly twisted around in my arms and lunged forward, indicating they didn't want to be held; they wanted to be put back on the ground so they could go on exploring the world on their own.

Slowly I learned to tell the difference between the hugs that were for them and the hugs that were for me. When I held them against their will, I wasn't expressing my affection for them; I was exercising my power over them, under the guise of love. There are the hugs that smother us and the hugs that liberate us. My job as a father wasn't to possess them, but to set them free.

I say that easily, as if I had been a model father who never tried to dictate the direction of his children's lives. But I can't make that claim. I wanted my oldest son to go to college. He balked, became a carpenter, and went on to build beautiful houses and a life of his own. My youngest daughter was facile with figures, so I urged her to study accounting. She became a conservation biologist; she spends her summers in a tent in the High Sierra, studying the connection between plants and birds.

I might argue that I acted out of love when I urged my children to live out my vision of their destiny. But I know now that I wasn't acting out of love; I was acting out of a sense of ownership, of dominion, which blinded me. It's a wise father who knows his children, and I can say that I didn't always know mine. If I had seen them clearly, I would have done more to encourage them to become the men and women they were born to be.

I have four children, and I am proud of them all, of what they have achieved despite my parental tendency to put my priorities ahead of theirs. I offered my advice; in their innate wisdom, they didn't heed it. If they had, it would have altered their nature, and that would have erected a barrier of resentment between us as impassable as the bars of a cage.

In midlife, when I found myself a bachelor again, I was drawn to a woman who had many endearing traits. I was attracted by the way she bounced around the tennis court, by the zestful way she moved, the spirited way she talked. In the beginning, it was a pleasure to be with her. She liked to sing; she liked to dance. But after a while, her arms around me felt less like an embrace than a stranglehold.

She had been through many relationships, all disastrous, including marriage to a man who had abandoned her. When we met, she was still reeling from that trauma. What she needed, what she wanted more than anything else was a man she could call her own, a husband whose presence she could count on every morning, every night. What I needed, what I wanted more than anything else at that moment of my life was time to be alone, time to adjust, time to devote myself to the work I wanted to do.

She began to refer to me as "my man" and couldn't understand why I objected to that term. One evening, at a small dinner party in her home, as I headed toward the kitchen, I heard her talking to her closest friend. She mentioned my name, then added, "the universe provides." As soon as she uttered those words, I felt the oppressive power of her love, and I knew we had to part. In time she found another man, one who was right for her, and I found a cottage by the sea.

I once saw a motto worked in needlepoint,

neatly framed and conspicuously hung on a kitchen wall. It read: "Where love rules, there is no will to power." I am surprised that after all these years those words come back to me so plainly. I see them again, as if they were indelibly imprinted on my brain, and for the first time I understand what they mean.

I believe in compassion; I believe in sharing; I believe in mates, partners, and friends helping each other on their sad and merry way through life. But I don't believe in dominion, in the right of one being to possess another, no matter what form that possession takes.

I believe our long human yearning for political liberty is rooted in our unquenchable desire to become the essential individuals we were meant to be. "I have sworn upon the altar of God, eternal hostility against every form of tyranny over the mind of man," Thomas Jefferson wrote, and we are stirred by his words without always knowing all they imply. We associate his battle cry with our aversion for czars, dictators, emperors, and kings who want to tell us what we can think and where we can go.

What we often fail to recognize is that remote rulers, no matter how despotic, generally exert less power over our lives than the ordinary people do, the people we live and work with every day. The latter are present, always present, with their own agendas and their own demands, which can oppress us unless we find the will within ourselves to resist.

A lovely woman comes into view. She is wearing a white polo shirt, jean shorts, and a yellow sweatshirt tied about her waist by the sleeves. With a start, I realize that she is not a part of my reverie, but here, now, with me on the beach.

The wind has shifted, and I didn't notice. The mist is blowing in from the sea. I rise and walk to the water's edge. As the woman draws alongside, she stops and comments on the sudden change in the air. We stand on the sand, chatting idly, and then she continues on her way. I watch her as she goes, watch the sway of her yellow shirt, and wonder if I have let an opportunity slip by.

The conversation, although brief, was effortless, and I know I could have kept it going if I had wanted to. I could have found out more about her. I could have asked if she would like a cup of coffee, and if she said yes, I could have taken her to a restaurant overlooking the water, where harbor seals sometimes break the placid surface and pelicans dive in plain view. We could have sat there talking quietly, finding out about each other, what we like, what we dislike, what sort of lives we lead.

But I didn't do any of those things, and I know that this wariness is an aspect of myself I must confront as I comb the sands of Miramar. It's not rejection that I fear—not at this juncture of my life. I'm not afraid if I asked her to join me for a cup of coffee that she would turn me down. What I fear is that she would accept, that acceptance would inevitably lead to involvement, and that at some point during the course of our involvement she would consider me her captive and try to make me over into someone I don't want to be.

It's an unfair assessment—I realize that. I know nothing about the woman, about what she values or how she might respond to the life I lead. For all I know, she may be as wary as I, and for the same reasons. If that is the case, then my fears aren't protecting me; they are keeping me from companionship.

I continue along the beach, trying to put the matter out of mind. But it is a disturbing thought—this idea that I may be standing in my own way. When I reach my beach house, I pour myself a cup of tea and carry it carefully through the sliding doors. I sit in a beach chair on the deck, thinking of the woman with the yellow shirt tied around her waist. She has disappeared in the thickening mist, and I will never know who she is.

six

tug-of-war

I sit on my deck late in the day, scanning the beach, watching the passersby. For a while I am blinded by the brilliance of the sun, which sets the sky aglow. When it finally drops below the horizon, I see the silhouette of a woman in the surf up to her waist, tugging on a rope.

There is a man with her, and he is standing higher up the beach in the soft, dry sand. I can hear her calling to him over the crash of the waves.

"Grab hold! If we pull together, we can get it out!" The man remains rooted in place, his arms folded across his chest.

A wave washes over the woman's pants, splashes her shirt, soaks her arms. The undertow almost sweeps her off her feet, but she hangs on. As the wave retreats, I can see the sharp angle of the rope as it slants under the sand. She tugs on the loose end, her body tense as she strains. Finally her strength gives out. She drops the rope, wades ashore, and falls to her knees, her head bowed. The breeze has died; in the still of evening, I can hear her sobs.

The man who has been standing by places a shawl around her shoulders. After a while she rises and they slowly walk away.

The evening gathers about me; the dusk settles in. But the image of the woman pulling on the loose end of a salt-soaked rope remains. I would paint her if I could, paint her as I saw her in the breakers, the spin-drift blowing through her stringy black hair, her drenched blouse clinging to her lean, unbending back. I would depict her struggle as epic, as I believe it was. I would show her desperation in the sinews of her body, in the hard, straight lines of her face and arms. I would put her figure off to one side of the painting, poised against the long slant of the rope, so that viewers would have no choice but to wonder what invisible counterweight lies buried in the sand.

I slump in a deck chair and close my eyes. I still see the woman plainly; I can't seem to let her go. I engage her in an imaginary conversation. I ask her if she knows what she is pulling against, and she tells me that she doesn't know, that it doesn't matter and she doesn't care. I ask her why she goes on pulling if it doesn't matter and she doesn't care. She doesn't answer. She goes on pulling, pulling with all the intensity of her being, against the unyielding object buried in the bed of the sea.

The contest that consumed her now consumes me. At some other moment of my life, I might have dismissed her behavior as eccentric, but now I understand her compulsion all too well. I feel as if she is an aspect of myself, a part of the past from which I have not yet fully emerged. I know her grim determination, the obsessive force that drives her on. She is convinced that if only she can pull harder, if only she can enlist the help of someone else, she will be able to wrest the rope free of the iron grip that holds it under the seafloor.

But she can't. No matter how hard she tries, she can't. I can feel the bone-deep despair that overwhelms her like a giant wave when at long last she is forced to admit that she can't.

I go to bed early, but I lie awake, watching the moon shadows on the wall. I'm weary now, more weary than I care to admit. In my weariness I have to recognize that I may have crossed that delicate boundary that separates the woman in the breakers from myself. Maybe all she saw was the loose end of a rope washing in the waves and she grabbed hold of it and tried to wrench it free, as if it was just a game. Maybe that's all it was, a game. But if it was just a game, why the cry for help and why the sobs when help never came?

It's hard to know what was going on. Maybe the event on the beach was staged; maybe it was a performance just for me. But I know what I saw, what I still see in my mind's eye, and I make my own conjectures out of my dark imaginings.

There is something down there, something the woman feels she must have. Maybe it's a father's approval, or a mother's affection, or a brother's recognition. Maybe it's a husband's touch, or a kind word from a friend. Maybe she wakes in the tender night and asks her lover to wrap his arms around her—and maybe her lover tells her he doesn't know how. So she tries to teach her lover how to love her, goes on night after night trying to teach him, but it's too late, for her lover is beyond loving, and all her effort is in vain.

In the dim light, I see the shadowy figure of the man again, see him standing by so patiently, waiting for her private tug-of-war to end. He doesn't offer to help; he doesn't urge her to stop. Is he wiser than she? Does he know what lies down there, buried in the sand? Perhaps he knows and is afraid to admit he knows, and so he makes his stand farther up the beach, apart.

I fall asleep, and in my sleep I dream. It's the same dream that has haunted my sleep since I arrived at Miramar. I am a young man again, employed by the New York public-relations firm I left two decades ago. I set out from my suburban home, board the commuter express for the city, but the train never arrives. I desperately need the job; I have a family to support, but the train never arrives.

Months go by. I am afraid my superiors will fire me. And then one morning I appear at the office, and my boss and fellow workers act as if I have never been absent, as if I have been doing my job all along. I try to work, to focus on the task at hand, but I can't. And the nightmare starts all over again. I dress, board the commuter express for the city, but the train never arrives.

The sound of the surf shatters my dream. I wake in the darkness, drenched with sweat. I step out on the deck, lean against the railing, and watch the white rushing foam of the sea.

"What's the matter with you?" I ask myself. "Why are you dreaming about a job you left so long ago?"

The question startles me, as if it were posed by someone other than myself. But there is no one with me in this middle night. The voice I hear is mine and mine alone, stirring up memories that go back to childhood.

When I was eight, my parents sent me to live with my grandparents. When my grandmother became ill, I was sent to live with my aunt and uncle. By then my father had died. My mother remarried and I was sent to live with her and my stepfather. Then my mother died and I was sent to my aunt and uncle again.

Through all these migrations I was never sure where I belonged. I was a child and I made the assumptions a child makes. I felt as if I was an outsider, a guest in somebody else's house. If I wanted to be taken care of, I thought I had to behave as a guest is supposed to behave. I had to avoid attracting attention to myself. I had to be compliant. I had to please the appointed guardians of my life. If I didn't, I was certain some terrible, nameless calamity might rise from nowhere and strike me down.

It wasn't as if my grandmother, my grandfather, my aunt, my uncle didn't have my best interests at heart. I'm sure they did. But they weren't my parents, their homes weren't my home, and that made all the difference in the way I lived as a boy and the decisions I made as a man.

When the time arrived for me to take care of myself, I didn't do what I wanted to do. I did what I had always done, what I thought others expected of me. Instead of investing in myself, in the course I wanted to take, whatever the risk, I opted for a job that provided a steady income and security. My aunt and uncle had always counseled prudence, and that seemed to me the prudent way. But it became the pivotal point of despair, the precise place where the nightmare began.

I possess this knowledge of myself now, but the knowing didn't come in a rush. It came gradually, over the course of years, and as it came, I found the will to alter the direction of my life. In time I gave up the white shirt and tie of the executive and donned the garb of the beachcomber. But I know now that, like the woman in the breakers, I still engage in a mighty tug-of-war.

I know where I want to be—and it's here on the sands of Miramar, where life comes full to me with every wash of the waves. As I walk the beach, I like to think I am an autonomous being, moving through the world as I wish to move, free of encumbrances. But despite my deepest yearnings, there is a contrary force, buried in some secret, shameful part of my being, drawing me toward conformity. I am still trying to meet the expectations of others, still afraid that if I don't, the whole unstable world will come down about my head.

So I am back there still—back at the job I thought I had left behind. I am there not by light of day, but by dread of night, in my dreams. I journey back to that alien land in my sleep, trying to set my wrongs aright, but the train never arrives.

This desire to please others, so widespread, so deeply rooted—I wonder where it comes from. Is it the result of what others do to us, or what we do to ourselves, absorbing the judgments that swirl about us when we are young, taking them in and making them our own? We yearn for a blessing from those who have the power to bestow it on us, and when they don't give us what we crave, we blame ourselves.

I know a seventy-year-old woman who is still waiting for a sign of love from her mother, who is ninety-five. The daughter calls faithfully once a week, inquiring about her mother's health, hoping for a kindly word in return, and almost always she hangs up on the verge of tears. But she goes on trying, endlessly trying, week after week, never conceding that the fault lies with her mother, not with her.

I listen to her lament as sympathetically as I can. I watch as she turns to her children, her friends, trying in vain to wrest from them the approval her mother withholds. My fervent hope is that one sleepless night she will suddenly understand that she is wasting a lifetime of energy in quest of something only she can supply.

The impoverished in spirit have no choice but to bless themselves. This is as true for my friend as it is for me, as it is for every individual who yearns for the affirmation they never had. We must bless ourselves; there is no other way. If we don't, there is no telling how far we will go or what terrible acts we will commit to prove our worthiness.

I am haunted by a story a journalist friend once told me. In a refugee camp in the Middle East, she spoke with a woman who held a baby in her arms. The mother proudly told my friend that the infant was a boy. She hoped to have many sons, she said—to give them to the revolution.

My friend never saw the woman again, but I can't help but conjecture about those sons and the martyrdom that came to them through mother's milk. I have to believe they grew up with their mother's mission on their minds, and that from an early age they were fully prepared to sacrifice their lives for the sole purpose of pleasing her. They undoubtedly convinced themselves that their deaths would advance a revolution—which wasn't their revolution until they were old enough to make it their own. But revolution wasn't the reason they shouldered their rifles or planted their bombs, killing others as they killed themselves. It was the justification, the rationale for their irrational deeds.

I wonder what might have happened if they had discovered within themselves the will to defy their mother, to let go of her expectations and act for themselves. Perhaps one had the makings of a teacher, another a poet, another a doctor, another a genuine peacemaker. Who can say what grand works they might have wrought if they had been allowed to live out their lives as they were meant to be lived?

For as long as I can remember, I have been drawn to the paintings of Georgia O'Keeffe without knowing why. I have often stood for hours in galleries and gazed at her pictures—so intense, so strikingly original: *New York Night, Cross by the Sea, Lake George Window, Cebolla Church, Pelvis with Moon, The White Trumpet Flower, The Lawrence Tree*. Only now, after all these years, am I beginning to understand the pull these paintings have for me. They are the works of a woman who dared to see with her own eyes.

As I move back inside my beach house, the faint rays of dawn are sifting through the windows, providing enough illumination for me to read by. I find the volume of reproductions that I have carried with me clear across the continent. I open to the page I know so well, a page that shows a pastel of a single dark alligator pear on a white cloth. But it's not the painting of the lush pear that I'm looking for: it's the artist's words that accompany it.

"I get out my work," O'Keeffe writes, "and have a show for myself before I have it publicly. I make up my own mind about it—how good or bad or indifferent it is. After that the critics can write what they please. I have already settled it for myself so flattery and criticism go down the same drain and I am quite free."

I am deeply affected by the directness of her words. What O'Keeffe writes and what she paints—they are one and the same. The individual who fears the criticism of others is no different from the one who seeks their praise. Both are shadow figures, fading into the landscape, lacking the will to act for themselves.

I can't help but think about what the world would have lost if O'Keeffe had felt otherwise. What if the artist in her had succumbed to the voices in her past—the knowing voices that must have been there—the voices that attempted to tell her which colors and shapes to live by and which to avoid? If she had heeded them, she would have died within herself, died in the spirit, if not in the flesh, and left no lasting testament of her passage through this world.

I am forever indebted to men and women like

O'Keeffe. I aspire to be as they were, as they are. In the aftermath of my nightmare, I feel as though I am closer to that moment of awakening than ever before. There is only one person who can sanctify my life. That power lies with me and me alone.

The light of morning has passed over the peaks of the coastal range and filled the sky. I leave my beach house, climb down the rickety steps from my deck, and head for the edge of the sea. I am lost in thought, moving by compulsion toward the exact place where I saw the woman in the breakers the night before. The loose end of the rope is still there; I can see it in the surf, floating free. It is a temptation—the way it washes in the waves. I feel as if I could wade in, grab hold, and yank it free. But I go on by.

seven

stone with a hole in the center

Far down the beach, I see a woman bending over, her head almost touching her toes, the strands of her windblown hair blending with the sand. She is wearing jeans and a white sleeveless T-shirt, and as I approach, she looks up at me and smiles.

"What are you looking for?" I ask.

"Stones with holes in them," she says. "I have a shelf full of them at home. A stone with a hole in the center wards off evil spirits."

"So how are you doing with evil spirits?"

"Lately—not so good," she replies.

I laugh and she laughs, too—but under her laughter I detect an earnestness. For her, this is more than a pastime, a momentary diversion on the beach. She believes in stones with holes in the center. If she didn't, why would she devote an entire shelf to them in her home?

I continue on my way, thinking about what she said, about what it means to me. I have my evil spirits, too. At night they invade my dreams; in the mornings they weigh me down.

I'm worried about money. My funds are dwindling. I no longer bother to balance my checkbook. Any day I expect a notice from my bank telling me they have closed my account because I'm so overdrawn. Suppose I become ill? I have no health insurance, no paid sick leave, no retirement income, none of the benefits that accrue to the workingman. Who will look after me?

I am alone, completely alone on this strip of beach. I want an antidote for my loneliness, a placebo I can swallow, a talisman I can hold to cast out my fears. I see a stone riddled with holes, half-buried in the sand. I pick it up—but even as I roll it over in my palm, I know it is too small to dispel the ache in my heart that grows larger with each passing day. I need a stone that is huge, a stone with a hole so big that it surrounds me body and soul.

I come upon a rock with a cavernous hole in the middle, carved out by the perpetual pounding of the waves. The rock is easily twice my height. It is perched at the edge of the beach, beside a bluff that rises straight up out of the sea. I crawl into the hollow and sit on a hard ledge, watching the breakers crash against the offshore reefs, sending plumes of spray into the air.

I sit as still as I can, my back straight; I make a valiant effort to empty my mind. I want to feel the cadence of the waves, the rise of the swells, the ebb of the tide. I want to move in unison with those elements, to become part of them as they become part of me.

I try to time my breathing with the wash of the waves, inhaling as a wave rolls up the beach, exhaling as it rolls back down. I concentrate on my breath because breath is the source of life. When I am aware of my breath, I am aware of myself and my place in the world.

I have a mantra, one that is distinctly my own—a high-pitched *wiiinnnd* that runs through the rigging of my mind. I say *wiiinnnd* as I inhale, *wiiinnnd* as I exhale, and then I start over again, trying to focus my attention on my breath, on the wind, on the waves. I tell myself that if I can breathe in and out ten times while intoning my mantra, I will have chased the evil spirits away.

It seems so simple. All I have to do is concentrate on my breathing through ten full cycles, hanging on to my single-syllable mantra, drawing out the word as I breathe. But try as I might, I can't master my malaise. My timing is off; I am out of step with the rhythm of the world. Long before I can complete the cycle, I lose track of the count and the evil spirits rush back in to fill the void.

It's the money, the insecurity, the loneliness, all the collective demons of my life, haunting my nights, haunting my days. It's ludicrous to think that I can sit here in a hole in a rock and make them go away. I'm not an Eastern mystic; I'm a Westerner by choice and birth, and my salvation lies in Western ways.

I want to rise and continue on my way, but some inner voice holds me here. Even though I have given up trying to measure my breath, I remain fixed inside this oval of stone, listening to the sound of the sea. I allow my mind to fill up with thoughts because that is what it wants to do. The universe is full of philosophies, and I'm open to any that drift my way.

I'm not immune to the crosswinds that sweep over the mountains and plains of the planet, bringing my thoughts to others and theirs to me. Those winds travel without respect for national boundaries, and they can't be halted by border guards. Despots and demagogues may attempt to stop the flow of ideas they fear, but there is no barricade high enough or wide enough to block the breeze.

The wisdom of the Zen master and poet Thich Nhat Hanh once reached me on such a wind, and I tucked it away in some remote recess of my mind. I believe we summon from buried memory what we need to know when we need to know it, and that is what happens to me now. Words from his book *The Miracle of Mindfulness* well up, seemingly from nowhere, as if I had been saving them for this precise moment of my life.

"People usually consider walking on water or in thin air a miracle," Nhat Hanh wrote. "But I think the real miracle is not to walk either on water or in thin air, but to walk on earth."

To the devout, his words may seem irreverent, maybe even sacrilegious, but I think they speak to the deepest spiritual impulses of men and women everywhere. When I think of saints, prophets, and poets, when I try to imagine what they are like and how they move through the world, I see them as individuals walking the earth with an awareness that sets them apart from ordinary men.

Gandhi was that way, so was Tolstoy, and so was Thoreau. St. Francis was that way; so was St. Joan. Jesus was surely that way, for we mark his journey through Galilee not by the distance he traveled, which wasn't vast, but by the intensity of what he did and said as he walked the land.

I don't know what made those people that way. Perhaps they paused long enough amid the tumult of life to listen to a voice within themselves that told them what to do and where to go. They didn't suppress that voice, smother it, push it down; they heeded it, obeyed it, followed its dictates—and as they did, the voice grew in power and strength, until it was the primary sound they heard.

Not all men are born to be saints, but I believe we are all born with a voice within that we tend to ignore until it becomes so indistinct we barely know it's there. The voice doesn't come from an almighty God in the sky; it comes from an in-dwelling God in the soul. The poet-philosopher Henri Bergson, author of *Creative Evolution*, called it the élan vital, the vital impulse, the divine spark, the life force that drives us on.

I find in the works of Bergson and Nhat Hanh a common meeting ground, a point where East and West are joined. When we walk the earth in a mindful way, we are fully conscious of ourselves, and when we are conscious of ourselves, we begin to climb the evolutionary scale, entering higher states of being than we have ever known before.

It's a crucial matter, this business of walking the earth in a mindful way, for it may be our only hope for raising the human race out of the morass of hostility and bloodshed that engulfs it now. What we are engaged in is nothing less than directing our own evolutionary destiny, ascending to a level of awareness where mayhem is no longer a way of life. That may sound like a miracle, and it is; but it is a miracle we can bring about through conscious effort, one man, one woman at a time.

I begin with myself: That is the starting point. I have it within my power to influence the course of history. If I act alone, it doesn't matter. It only matters that I act. If two act, so much the better. If a hundred or a thousand or a million act, that is better yet. Our separate acts will in time become a collective adaptation, and we will become a saner species than we are.

But that's not my prime motivation at this moment of my life. I'm not trying to save the world; I'm trying to drive my evil spirits away. Maybe those two objectives aren't as far apart as they seem. Maybe the personal and political, the private and public, are mirror images of each other. When the demons vanish, so does the destruction.

Where to begin—that's what I must think of now. The stone I'm sitting on is wet and cold, and so am I. But if I leave now, I know I will be attacked at once by the same old furies. They are out there waiting like swarming gnats and stinging nettles. A suit of armor would protect me from the onslaught, but it would also weigh me down.

I have often heard it said that alienation is the

curse of the modern world, but I think it is the curse of mankind and his inquisitive mind, going all the way back to Adam and Eve. Our forebears bit deeply into the apple of knowledge, and that is where our alienation began. Instead of accepting paradise as it was given to us, we examined it atom by atom, we built cities of concrete and cars of steel and we stripped the earth for its fossil fuels. I don't deny we benefited in many ways from our industry. But where is the Garden of Eden? Where is the music of the spheres?

No other animal is as divorced from its habitat as we. If we are estranged from the land we live on, then we are estranged from the life we lead and at war with ourselves. And the bodies strewn across the landscape aren't bodies at all. They are the living dead, the hollow men with eyes that don't see and ears that don't hear.

I am surprised at myself. I stepped into this rock with a hole in the center, intending to calm myself down. Instead, I have worked myself up to a fever pitch of agitation. Maybe that is how it's supposed to be. Who says meditation brings serenity? Perhaps its purpose is to shake off sleep, to stir the blood, to rouse the mind. It's midday now, but I am more awake than I was when I left my bed at dawn.

I hear voices, the laughing voices of children at play. As I leave the rock I see that I share this stretch of beach with a family of picnickers. The adults are huddled around a hibachi; I can smell the smoking coals and sizzling meat. The children are racing down to the water's edge and dashing back up again, tumbling over each other as they go.

There is a verity in the scene, a universality. Why do people all over the world flock to the sandy shore? I think it's because the instant they touch the sand, the moment they hear the surf, the evil spirits flee and they feel at home in the world.

I move slowly, deliberately, over the sand, aware that the universe is not a hostile place. "Drink your tea slowly," Nhat Hanh wrote. "There is a great rush in our world to get things over and done with, but there is no reverence for the work itself." What I need now is to immerse myself in life—to express my reverence for the moment at hand, the moment in which I dwell, and for the beachcombing I want to do.

I follow the line of the tide along the beach, studying each shell, each scrap of shell, until I see it distinctly in the glistening sand. I bend over and pick up a fragment that has washed ashore. It's the skeleton of a purple sea urchin, its surface an array of imbedded beads. I close my eyes. I lift the shell to my ears, my nose. I rub my hand across its tiny globes, gathering its message through my fingertips like a blind man reading braille.

eight

the motions of the world

I start my van and travel down the winding Coast Highway, the ocean on my right. My vehicle is old and wheezy and it balks like a mule when going up a hill. In my rearview mirror I see a young man at the wheel of his red sports coupe, with a young woman beside him and a surfboard neatly balanced on the roof. He wants to pass, but there is precious little room on the narrow road and nothing I can do. He pulls out across the double yellow line, blaring his horn, and makes an obscene gesture as he races by, nearly taking off my front fender as he cuts back in. I am badly shaken.

A mile or so farther along, I turn into a side road and park on a grassy shoulder overlooking a salt-marsh preserve. I sit there for a while, quietly collecting myself, studying the eucalyptus forest in the distance, and, closer in, the coastal estuary, the brackish ponds and mud flats. When I am sufficiently calmed down, I string my field glasses around my neck and enter this tranquil habitat, this sanctuary for all manner of wildlife, including me.

I stop on a wooden footbridge that spans a narrow waterway and listen to the harsh buzz of a marsh wren hidden in the reeds. A snowy egret wades in the shoals, spearing prey with his sharp black bill. Bank swallows twist and turn in miraculous flight over my head, catching insects on the wing. Cinnamon teal take off from the muddy embankment—and far off, a black-shouldered kite perches silently on a post and waits.

All these species, and so many more, dwell together in this one fertile oasis without getting in each other's way. Yes, the egret feeds on frogs and fish, the swallows devour mosquitoes, and the kite kills snakes and rodents whenever it can. Sometimes the peregrine falcon swoops down and snatches a duck out of the sky. But those are not acts of cruelty; they are the way of survival in a natural world. What is cruel is the unnatural way we humans behave toward each other.

I think again of the young man in the red sports coupe, of his insulting gesture and his infuriating attempt to force me off the road. I think, too, of the young woman at his side, laughing at his recklessness as if it were a virtue, and of how that spurs him on. Each time she laughs, his foot presses harder on the gas pedal and the car spurts ahead, gaining on the car in front, which he must pass, because if he doesn't, the woman at his side may start to wonder if he really is the man he wants her to think he is.

I wonder if he knows where he's heading, or how, or why—this young man rushing toward his grave. He's so sure he's veering south, past farms of artichokes, past fields of sheep grazing on the barren slopes above the sea. He's so certain that he is the center of the universe, that he is in control of all he surveys, when in fact he is no more than a flyspeck on a planet hurtling through the sky.

When I was young, I read a poem called "This Dim and Ptolemaic Man," by John Peale Bishop, and the lines come back to me now. In his poem, Bishop depicts a farmer who saves enough money to buy a rattly Ford and how he feels "motion spurt beneath his heels" as he drives hell-bent down the road:

Morning light obscures the stars.
He swerves avoiding other cars,
Wheels with the road, does not discern
He eastward goes at every turn

Nor how his aged limbs are hurled
Through all the motions of the world,

How wild past farms, past ricks, past trees,
He perishes toward Hercules.

For a long time after I read the poem, the line "He eastward goes at every turn" kept reeling through my brain, an enigma. Why is the farmer going eastward? At last the answer dawned on me. He is going eastward because the earth is turning eastward; he is a traveler on the spinning planet, even if he is too self-absorbed in his new-bought car to feel himself being "hurled through all the motions of the world."

The poem intrigues me because of the title: the way the poet joins "dim and Ptolemaic" to describe the egocentric nature of man. Ptolemy, the ancient astronomer, declared that earth was a motionless body and that sun, moon, and planets revolved around it at varying speeds. That view remained fixed in the minds of men for more than a thousand years—until a wiser astronomer named Copernicus came along. Copernicus said that the earth was moving, rotating on its axis, orbiting the sun along with the other planets. He reasoned that because man was moving with the earth, he couldn't sense the movement at all.

But Copernicus sensed it—I have to believe he did. I believe he knew he was a passenger on the planet, that he was traveling with the earth through the heavens, long before his calculations proved that he was right and Ptolemy wrong. I am convinced that scientists like Copernicus are the painters and composers of the spheres. Like all artists, they begin with their hunches, conjectures, and speculations—which arise from what they sense—and then they create the painting and the music so that the rest of us can see and hear.

Galileo, gazing through his telescopes, constructed an even more detailed picture of the universe than Copernicus, and in so doing enraged the religious zealots of his day. They forced him to recant his theories and imprisoned him in his own house, under pain of death, until he died. I find it ironic that Galileo, who understood so well the motions of the world, was restricted in his travels, while the dim and Ptolemaic churchmen of the Inquisition walked freely about the streets, never realizing that they were "perishing toward Hercules."

Four centuries have come and gone since the Holy Office put Galileo on trial for saying that the earth moves. But I have to ask myself what separates the zealots of the Inquisition from the fanatics who drive the Coast Highway in their turbocharged cars today. Their styles may differ, but their perspective is the same. They know nothing of the workings of the earth and how it turns. They cling to their notion that the world exists for them, and they are perfectly willing to run over anyone who gets in their way.

I have a conviction—one I can't prove, but I believe it anyhow. I believe there is a clock within me, a living clock, and it keeps pace with the pulse beat of the world. I hear the slow ticktock of the planet when I stand in a salt marsh or walk the sands of Miramar, and I lose it the instant I slip behind a steering wheel. The moment I exceed the speed at which I was born to move, I lose the tempo of the natural world and become like a singer who has lost the rhythm of his song.

What science gives, the combustion engine takes away. The former tells us what the universe looks like; the latter numbs us to what we see. The faster we travel, the less we know. It's as if speed itself is an infectious disease, deadly not only because of the mangled bodies that lie by the side of the road but also because of the impenetrable barrier it erects between ourselves and our world.

My thoughts are broken by a small bird that persists in paddling back and forth under the footbridge where I stand. He swims, half-submerged, and I follow him from one side to the other, leaning over the wooden railing for a better look. Although I have stood waiting and watching in this same place many times in the past, I can't recall seeing this particular species before. I note the black ring around his thick bill; that is something of a giveaway. I recall seeing a bird with that distinctive marking in my field guide.

A man appears farther along the path, emerging from the bulrushes and pickleweed. He has a great shock of white hair and a face so bronzed he looks as if he has been out in the sun since the day he was born. He is moving quickly, with a purpose; he has a spotting scope on a tripod braced across his shoulder. He stops beside me and watches the ducklike bird that suddenly dives and pops up like a cork about fifty feet away.

"A pied-bill grebe?" I ask.

"Yes," the man says with the assurance of one who knows.

I ask him if he has seen anything else of interest, and he rattles off about twenty species, several of which I didn't know were in the marsh and a few I never heard of before. He announces that he has been up since dawn, driving from ocean to bay, harbor to redwood forest, creek to reservoir, and that he has seen 136 species so far. He says he has one more site to visit, a slough about twenty miles down the coast, where he hopes to find at least fifteen more species, raising his bird count to more than 150 for the day.

I watch as he rushes off, wondering if he will reach the slough in time to meet his goal, for he will soon lose the daylight. One hundred and fifty different birds! I wonder if it's possible to see, really see, that many species in a single day.

I turn back to the pied-bill grebe. I watch him for ten, fifteen, twenty minutes. When I feel I know him well, I leave the marsh and climb a sandy bluff, arriving at the top as the underrim of the sun touches the unbroken line of the sea.

I watch the sun drop below the horizon. It sinks quickly, and I suddenly know that I have been as dim and Ptolemaic as the farmer in his rattly Ford. For the first time in my life I am fully aware of the speed at which I am traveling through the air. The sun is not setting; the earth is spinning away. In a matter of minutes it has pitched eastward a distance equal to the diameter of the sun. And I am going eastward with it, going eastward through the night, through the day.

It occurs to me that perhaps the purpose of a sunset is to sweep self-delusion away. I have no sense of motion when the sun is overhead, hanging in the sky. At high noon, earth and sun appear to be absolutely still. Even as the sun slips down, I feel as though I am standing on a stationary planet. But when I see how the horizon rises to swallow the sun, I realize how I have allowed myself to be deceived.

It's dark when I arrive at my beach house. I

drag a mattress out on the deck and lie on my back, watching the moon. I have been watching it carefully ever since I arrived at Miramar, trying to solve its mystery. We have dispatched astronauts to its surface, and for a while that seemed like such an enormous feat. But now that the wonder of the moon landing has worn off, it seems more like a circus stunt, like so many clowns tumbling out of a tiny car, and the moon itself remains as elusive as before.

Tonight, the moon is as full and bright and yellow as I have ever seen it. It appears to be climbing up the eastern sky; right now it's suspended over the crest of the coastal range. It looks to me as if the moon is following the path of the sun, traveling from east to west, but I know that is self-deception, too. Earth and moon are both eastbound—except the earth and I are moving faster, so it seems as if the moon is going the other way.

It's late when I fall asleep. I'm awakened early by the shattering sounds and noxious fumes of Jet Skis. I stand on my deck, surveying the ocean, watching the noisy machines bounce over the breakers like seagoing snowmobiles. They gather below my beach house, where they multiply: two, then four, then eight, then twelve. The riders stand straight up in the cockpit and drive directly into the swells; they vault over the crests and reverse direction in midair.

One of the riders is thrown from his perch like a cowboy from a bucking bronco. He does a double flip before crashing headfirst into the sea. I assume he has broken his neck—but no, I see him swimming through the surf in pursuit of his runaway machine, which is going in circles. He catches up, clambers back aboard, revs up the engine, and plows into an oncoming wave.

I wonder about these riders of the surf and the lengths to which they go to breathe excitement into their lives. They are overcome with a sense of power because they have planted a combustion engine between their legs that enables them to leapfrog over the waves. I would like to hail them ashore and tell them what I have so recently learned.

I would tell them that if they want thrills, they should throw away their toys and ride the greatest roller coaster of all, the earth on which they dwell. And I would tell them that it will cost absolutely nothing because they gained admission free of charge on the day they were born.

nine

the raven and the radar

A thing of beauty is a joy forever:
Its loveliness increases; it will never
Pass into nothingness; but still will keep
A bower quiet for us, and a sleep
Full of sweet dreams, and health, and quiet breathing.

—*John Keats*

I wake early, filled with resolve. I skip breakfast and take to the beach, determined to investigate the mystery that has bothered me since I arrived at Miramar. I see it now, as I see it every morning from my deck—a spherical antenna that rises like a giant mushroom from the headland about a mile away. I have decided to get as close to it as I can and find out for myself exactly what it is doing there.

I have asked many people what it is, but they shrugged their shoulders or stared at me blankly and said they didn't know. Their indifference surprised me, for the antenna is the dominant landmark along this stretch of coast, towering over the bluff on which it stands.

I pass through the harbor and follow a dirt path that comes to an abrupt end at a paved road. I step over a guardrail and start up a steep incline. Almost at once I confront blazing red capital letters on a sign:

WARNING

U.S. Air Force Installation

It is unlawful to enter this area without permission of the Installation Commander.

Sec. 21, Internal Security At of 1950.

While on this installation, all personnel and the property under their control are subject to search.

I continue on up the hill until I reach a chain-link fence with barbed wire across the top, encircling the installation, blocking access from sea or land. Beyond the fence, I can plainly see the enormous dish, two smaller antennae, and several low buildings. Suddenly a door to one building opens and a heavyset woman in a khaki uniform strides toward me.

"Can I help you?" she asks firmly from her side of the fence.

"I'm just curious," I say. "What is this place, anyhow?"

"This is a radar station. We track missiles fired from Vandenberg Air Force Base."

"Vandenberg Air Force Base! That's four hundred miles away!"

"That's correct."

"Where do the missiles land?"

"Way out in the Pacific. Near an atoll. And now I must warn you that you're trespassing on Air Force property."

I would like to ask more questions, but her manner makes it clear that our conversation has come to an end.

"I'm sorry," I say. "I didn't know."

As I turn to leave, I see two surfers about fifty yards off to my right, skirting the installation. They are hiking up the headland in their wet suits, their boards under their arms. I follow them along a well-worn trail until they disappear over the edge of the embankment. When I arrive at that point, I stand for a moment, taking in the sweep of the rocky coast. Below me, at the base of a steep path, is a pocket beach, by far the most beautiful of any I have come upon since I began hiking the sands of Miramar.

When I reach it, I find myself in a land apart, an enclave, the kind of place one seldom discovers through conscious effort, only stumbles on while searching for something else. To the north, the rugged point of land juts into the sea. To the south, sea lions bask on sunbaked rocks. Behind me the escarpment rises, a sheer wall undercut by the ceaseless action of the ocean. Beyond the breakers, the surfers kneel on their boards, rising and falling with the swells.

I stretch out on the sand, my hands under my head, and look up, expecting to see the deep blue dome of heaven. But what I see is the radar antenna, standing between me and the sun, casting its shadow over the sand. From this perspective, it appears even more imposing. I can see the whole of it—the supporting structure that ties it to the headland, the powerful swivel neck, the vast concave dish aimed straight up at the sky.

If I were a landscape artist, a Turner or a Constable, I would paint the scene from this angle, from the beach below. I would paint the breakers, the surfers on their boards, the sea lions on the rocks, and I would paint the antenna high up on the bluff, overlooking it all. I would not omit it from the painting for the sake of prettiness. I would paint it as it is. I would paint it not as a thing of beauty but as it appears, a blemish on the landscape, an object intrusive on this isolated point of land.

I feel the anger rising within me. I remember a tree-shaded house on a winding country road. I was sitting at my typewriter, looking out a window through a grove of oaks and maples, when a crew of electric-utility workers pulled up in a truck. As I watched, they began to drill a hole at the edge of my front yard. I rushed out and asked the foreman what was going on. He told me he was going to put up a pole supported by guy wires with cables strung across the top.

"You can't do that," I said. "I don't want to look at an ugly pole every time I look out my window."

The foreman waved his hand. "People always say that, but after a while they don't even notice anymore."

I have never forgotten those words.

The Air Force generals who had a radar station built on this headland understood the truth of that statement. They withstood the protests of those who saw the huge antenna as a desecration, a blight on the beauty of the coast. They knew that in time the structure would become a part of the passing scene, and that eventually people would view it as if it belonged, as if it had always been there.

I know how it happens; I have done it myself many times. A few months ago a crass billboard suddenly appeared on the Coast Highway. I wrote irate letters of protest; I was so upset, I wanted to sneak up to it in the middle of the night and saw it down. Almost any act, lawful or not, seemed justified. The weeks went by and, as the foreman predicted, the sign became less obtrusive. One day I drove past the billboard, and it wasn't until I was miles down the highway that I realized I hadn't even seen it there.

But now, as I sit on the beach under the shadow of the antenna, I wonder about the price I paid. I believe I have an inalienable right to the beauty of the earth created long before I was born. But I sense that each time I succumb to ugliness, to the base and profane in my surroundings, I give up a piece of my birthright, and a quintessential part of my being dies.

The people who betray the land—they see my ability to adapt to ugliness as a portent of progress, an auspicious sign. But I see it as a character flaw, a way of deadening my senses, of reducing myself to an automaton.

I am not opposed to progress. I understand the role of productivity in creating mass wealth and leisure, and I have the greatest respect for the work of research scientists and development engineers. As a journalist, I have observed the construction of bridges, dams, and highways. I have witnessed the white heat of the steelworker's furnace; I have reported on the way supercomputers would alter mankind's view of the world.

But I am convinced that we know not what we do when we assign a higher priority to the products of our technology than to the natural beauty of the land. It seems to me as if ugliness is a social disease, one we inflict upon ourselves, and it consumes us in our entirety a little at a time. We have been given this Garden of Eden, this land of milk and honey, and bit by bit we are letting it slip away.

I believe the desire for beauty is built into me, as it is built into everyone, and that our lifelong quest for it is our greatest and most important morality play. *Beauty* is the antonym of *violence*, the antidote for all the pent-up rage in the world. We have this choice—we can opt for beauty or we can opt for violence. If we choose violence, then death and destruction will be our reward. If we choose beauty, we will create a bower of quiet for our children, and for ourselves a sleep full of sweet dreams.

The sun is directly over the radar station, glinting off the steel; I can feel the warmth of it on my face and arms. I rise to my feet, pulling the peak of my cap farther down my forehead to shade my eyes. As I do, I notice for the first time that the beach about me is littered with beer cans. I count them—there are more than thirty strewn about, lying every which way, some exposed, others partially buried in the sand.

I remember a few years ago hiking with a geologist friend, Lex Blood, five miles up the Grinnell Trail in Glacier National Park. Below us spread a pale blue lake, a glacial tarn; above us rose "the Garden Wall," the Continental Divide. About halfway up, Lex saw a white object stuffed in a rocky crevice. He poked it loose with a stick and stuffed it in a pocket inside his backpack.

"What is it?" I asked.

"A snot rag!" he snapped.

The rugged mountains all around us were a place of awe, a veritable storehouse of information about the history of our world. But to one hiker on the rugged trail, they were no more than a handy depository for a piece of tissue paper on which he had blown his nose. I can still hear the moral indignation in Lex's voice; I can still see the outrage in his eyes.

I know exactly how he felt, because I feel that way now. I am infuriated by these empty cans, disillusioned by the abuse, the flagrant insensitivity to the beauty of the land. And yet, despite the evidence all about me, I can't let go of my conviction that the quest for beauty is as inherent in the individuals who littered this beach as it is in me, as it is in every woman, every man.

Why do they do it? Why do they carry their beer cans to this lovely, isolated beach when they could just as easily sit on a city curb or beside a garbage dump? I believe they do it because they have no choice. They are drawn to the beauty of this place; this is where they have to be.

But when their party is over, it's as if some imp of the perverse takes over—as if they have to prove to others, to their friends, their peers, that they are immune to the force of nature that lured them here. To behave otherwise would be a tacit admission that they feel a connection to the land, an attachment to sea and sand, a bond with what they perceive as sacred in the world.

A genuine expression of reverence seems to be something they can't afford. I see the results of their repression in the litter they leave behind. These empty cans scattered about my feet speak to me with a power that transcends words. They tell me that those who made this mess are in rebellion against themselves.

I live in a time and place that puts a premium on hardheadedness. I know a man who constantly ridicules his wife's desire to go down to the beach at dusk and watch the sunset. "Women love sunsets," he says derisively. He wants to be seen as a practical fellow, a pragmatic man of business. And perhaps he is. But I can't help thinking that this pragmatic man he purports to be is merely an identity he has chosen for himself, a protective coating that comes between him and how he feels, truly feels, in those rare moments when he lets himself.

I can see little difference between those who say they are indifferent to sunsets and those who travel to the beach and litter it with empty cans. Both are attracted to beauty; both are afraid of what others will think if they admit that it is so. Both have a vested interest in appearing cool and tough. In their view, it is the cool and tough who inherit the world.

But that strikes me as a destructive approach to life, one founded on self-denial, which is a form of suicide. I am wary of those who suppress their desires, who are deprived of beauty either by choice or circumstance, for I never know at what moment they will explode.

I think of the multitudes pressed into the ghettos of the world. They see no green hills, no grazing sheep, no flowering meadows, no soaring birds. Day after day they walk the pavement and stare at the stark walls. Separated from all that is natural, they suddenly strike out wildly, looting and razing, smashing windows, overturning cars. They rampage through the streets, consumed with rage, never realizing that what they want most, what they miss most, is what they never had. It is the absence of beauty that drives them mad.

My early memories of childhood are at my grandparents' house in Manhattan Beach where there were dahlia gardens, mulberry trees, and a clear view of the sea. I lived with my parents on the West Side of New York, and I can remember how the absence of beauty affected me. The desire to escape the hard, cold city streets governed my every thought; it led to a rift with my parents that never healed. I pleaded with them to move; they couldn't. Citybound, they remained in their apartment—and shipped me to live with Grandma and Grandpa.

The arrangement had a logic to it, especially from my father's point of view. He made fashion drawings for department stores, advertising agencies, and magazines, and he wanted to be near the clients he served. But when he finished his work, he would set a canvas on his easel and paint in oils with a palette knife. He painted the white birches and rocky ledges of the Maine coast. He painted an Indian squaw holding her papoose, both wrapped in a long red shawl. He painted Moorish harbors, and a lateen-rigged dhow floating across the Arabian Sea. He painted out of his imagination sights he had never seen.

I lost all those paintings in a house fire years ago, but they remain vividly etched in my memory. I realize now that they reveal an aspect of my father's nature I didn't know—his longing for a different landscape, one with softer lines and brighter hues. If I could meet him now, I would ask him the question that haunts me.

You lived in the city, I would say, but you didn't paint the city. So why did you stay in the city when your heart was somewhere else?

I long for his answer, but I hear only the sounds of the sea.

I glance up at the radar station, momentarily shrouded in mist. When the fog clears, I see that the antenna has moved. The massive dish, which had been facing the sky, has rotated on its axis so that it is tilted toward the sea. I assume it has been positioned so that it can track missiles now being fired.

I find myself upset. I want someone to talk to. In my frustration, I imagine picking up where I left off in my conversation with the guard at the radar station.

Why are you doing this? I challenge her.

We track missiles, she tells me. That is what we're here for. That is what we do.

But why?

Because we must protect ourselves against our enemies.

But my enemies aren't your enemies, I tell her. My enemies are those who want to defend me by destroying what I love.

If you don't defend what is yours, she says, someone stronger than you will come and take it away.

I want so desperately to make her understand. I want her to see that beauty is the cause of peace, that missiles are the cause of war.

Don't you know, I say, *that we can't put an end to human hostility by appropriating a headland and putting an antenna on top of it. We can't create a peaceful world by building missiles and tracking them across a thousand miles of open sea. There is only one way we can create a peaceful world, and that is by bringing beauty—the beauty of art, the beauty of nature—to people everywhere, because that is what they crave. Each time we remove a portion of beauty from the world, we diminish ourselves.*

Spent with effort, filled with the futility of words, I let the image fade.

The time has come to leave. I climb the steep path to the top of the bluff, where I pause for a moment to survey the vast expanse of the ocean. Below, I hear the hoarse croak of a raven. I see him soaring on ragged wings along the ridge. He lands on a ledge and flutters into his nest, a hole in the cliff, no more than it needs to be. I gaze at the place where he disappeared; I can barely see it. The essential character of the raven's nest lies in its invisibility, in the way it blends with all the shadows and colors of the world.

I leave the headland and head for home, thinking that if I could choose between the way of the raven and the way of man, I would choose the way of the bird.

ten

the stone skimmers

Midmorning—and the sun is so bright and glorious in the sky I can barely remember all the past days of windblown fog. A faint onshore breeze, cooled by the Japanese current, brushes my face, the light caress of a woman in the wind. As I walk the beach, I feel as if a great weight has been lifted from me, and I am ready to reach out beyond the boundaries of myself.

Far down the beach, I come upon two men—one gray-haired and the other balding—throwing stones into the sea. They are walking slowly, talking as they walk, pausing every few steps to search for another stone. When they find one, they fling it sidearm across the shallow water, watching it sink or hop.

As I watch them, I am overcome by an irresistible urge. I find a flat skimmer, worn smooth by the waves, and skip it across the calm surface of the sea. It hops three times. I am filled with delight; I haven't lost the knack acquired so long ago.

As soon as one stone sinks, I look for another, then another. I pick up a near-perfect stone, one as round and thin as a blade. It skips five times. I don't know how many decades have gone by since I skipped a stone five times.

I remember my oldest son, when he was only three or four, picking up stones and throwing them into a lake. I told him to stop; it didn't do any good. Whenever I turned my back, he would pick up another stone and fling it into the water. Years later I walked with my grandsons beside that same lake and watched them throw stones, just as their father had. I didn't try to interfere; by then I knew the futility of that. It is no more possible to keep boys from throwing stones than it is to keep dogs from barking or cats from arching their backs.

I don't know where the impulse comes from—if I do it because it's instinctive or because it gives me so much joy. Didn't St. Paul caution the Corinthians to abstain from the kind of behavior that engages me now? "When I was a child," he wrote in his first epistle, "I spake as a child, I understood as a child, I thought as a child: but when I became a man, I put away childish things."

I once had a Sunday school teacher who preached those lines with all their gospel force. He had long before put away childish things and wanted the children under his tutelage to do the same. "When you grow up," he said, "you will see through different eyes." Now I am grown up; now it seems to me as if he misused the words of St. Paul. I don't want to suppress the child in me; I want to preserve the child in me.

The two men who had been throwing stones turn and trudge through the heavy sand. They pass over the dunes; for a while I can see their heads bobbing on the other side. I study the dunes, squinting, seeing for the first time the way they are shaped in the mind's eye by subtle hues. I have passed this way many times, but I have never before seen so many shades of pink, rose, and ocher.

Beyond the dunes, the houses appear crunched together and suspended in air like toy dwellings on a tiny stage. It could be a scene in a painting by Henry Miller. I came upon his art in a gallery down the coast at Big Sur. I was familiar with Miller as a writer, the ultimate expatriate and chronicler of bohemian life, a man of hard-bitten prose, which often lapsed into diatribe. But I did not know him as a watercolorist, an adult who saw the world as a child sees it, a fantastical world of bulbous noses, cockeyed hats, and floating houses—all painted with exuberance, as if he had put his vision to paper in one great flourish.

One of my favorite Miller paintings is of Jerusalem—the Old City with its skyline of mosques and minarets in splashes of red and blue, green, gray, and copper. Everything in the painting is suggested; nothing explained. In its innocence it is like the work of a third grader, the kind one might see tacked to a classroom wall, except it is far superior because it has the passionate intensity, the spontaneity and skill of an artist who is still a boy.

I bought a book of Miller's reproductions and I often browse through it, absorbing his clowns, sailboats, villages, his portraits of friends and family members. What astonishes me most, apart from the wonder of his work, is the generous spirit that underlies it all. Some paintings he sold for a pittance; the bulk he gave away. A friend might say, *Henry, I love that painting of a man with a bird*, and Henry would reply, *Here, it's yours.*

For Miller to paint as he painted, to live as he lived, he had to be totally free of the paralyzing fear that seeps into the marrow of most men's bones as they mature. "When I write, I work," Miller says. "But when I paint, I play." And therein lies the simple secret of his artistry. His paintings reveal a mind that was running free all the time. The title of a book of his paintings is *Paint as You Like and Die Happy*.

At another moment in my life, I might have taken that statement as a dare, but now it strikes me as a moral imperative. I feel as if I have spent a large chunk of my life abiding by rules and regulations set forth by others; but now I am concerned about how I will feel as I lay dying about the life I have lived.

I continue down the beach, humming softly, not thinking about the tune. The melody just seems to be there, in my head and on my lips, and I don't know why. The lyrics rise from a distant memory.

Why do I love you?
Why do you love me?
Why should there be two
Happy as we?

And I suddenly find myself singing aloud, singing at the very top of my voice. The music is by Jerome Kern, the words by Oscar Hammerstein, the song from *Show Boat*. I am no longer an adult walking the beach; I am a child in the perfumed bedroom of my buxom great-aunt, Leona Libby Lewis, who sang in vaudeville. She is well along in years, but her voice is still deep and resonant. She stops for a moment and looks at me, sitting on a stool beside her, overwhelmed.

"Sing, Ricky, sing!" she orders.

"I can't sing," I reply. I mean that I can't sing in tune, which is what I have been told over and over again, until I am convinced that it is true.

She is outraged. "Come over here," she says. "Stand next to me." She reaches out, puts her arms around me, draws me close. "Now sing," she demands. "Sing with me!"

I hear the power of her voice; it encompasses me. I open my mouth and push out the words, hoping they match the tune.

"Louder," she says.

I push harder.

"Sing the words! Sing the words! Don't be afraid!"

I sing louder, and louder still.

Can you see the why or wherefore
I should be the one you care for . . .

The melody rises and swirls around the room, filling the empty spaces, rattling the chandelier. "Who says you can't sing?" Aunt Leona cries. "Don't ever say that you can't sing!"

The music remained long after my aunt

Leona let me go, but the fear returned and I seldom sang again. In later years, whenever I tried, the people around me—my wife, my children—would look at me askance and belittle my efforts. A family rule was set down: Daddy is not allowed to sing at the dinner table. Intended, I suppose, at least partially as a joke, it had a deadening effect all the same. What I really wanted was for them to lift their voices and sing with me.

If you sing with me, I wanted to say, I can follow your lead and sing in tune.

But I didn't ask; I was too afraid. I listened to the music I loved. I sang in my head, inside my being. I heard the chords deep down in my soul. But I didn't sing aloud. The fear came between me and the melody, and I repressed my song.

Until now.

The beach is deserted—but even if it were filled with people, I doubt I would be deterred. I hear my voice carrying over the breakers, as if Aunt Leona were urging me on.

I'm a lucky boy,
You are lucky, too,
All our dreams of joy
Seem to come true. . . .

The song is a duet. I am singing to a woman, and she is singing to me. Our voices blend and part and blend again. All at once the day is filled with possibility. I believe that if I sing in this way, without fear, I can hit the notes exactly right and make her materialize. I have no idea who the woman is, but that doesn't matter. What does matter is this sudden sense of lightness, of liberation, born of song.

We yearn so for this lightness in our everyday lives and rarely find it because of the fear, instilled by others, that we will miss a note, skip a beat, sing off-key. Rather than belt it out, we squelch our song. I have seen the results of that repression, seen how it sears the spirit and withers the flesh, making us old before our time.

A while back I visited a relative, who in my childhood memory is spiritedly playing the piano. She showed me around her house, stopping at the entryway to the living room. The couch and chairs were wrapped in thick, clear plastic covers. It was as though the room were a period piece in a museum, cordoned off by an invisible braided rope.

Impulsively, I crossed the imaginary barrier, and as I did, I felt the tension in the air. I sensed at once that I had violated a strict house rule, but I wanted to look at the piano—a stately, well-waxed spinet she had inherited from her mother—standing in a corner. I tried to lift the cover clamped down over the keyboard, but it was locked or stuck fast, like the lid of a trunk that hadn't been pried open in years.

She was watching me closely, her face drawn, her bare arms crisscrossed over her chest, her shoulders hunched, her fingers digging into her skin, as if she were hugging herself to ward off a chill.

"Do you still play?" I asked.

"Oh no," she replied. "I haven't touched it in years."

"That's too bad."

She stood in silence for a long time, then said, "I would give it to my daughter, but she's so careless with things."

A bitter wind swept through the house. I ended the visit as quickly as I could. I boarded a plane; on the long flight home, at forty thousand feet above sea level, her words kept whirring through my head.

Sometime afterward, I attended a concert by the great Russian cellist Mstislav Rostropovich in a small city in central Michigan. Before he began to play, he held up his Stradivarius so the audience could see the gash on the face of his instrument. He explained in the most charming and childish manner how the gash was there when he acquired it, how it had been inflicted by a previous owner in an accident a century earlier, and how it gave the cello its distinctive tone and character. Then he put bow to strings. A hush fell over the audience as the sweet, vibrant sound of the scarred cello filled the room.

Afterward, at a reception in the boardroom of the corporation that had sponsored the concert, Rostropovich sat in a comfortable chair while his long-haired dachshund squirmed on his lap and crawled up his sleeve. A public-relations man popped his head through the door. "Do you want a newspaper for that dog?" he asked. "What for?" the cellist replied. "He can't read."

Rostropovich had played that same theme on a grander scale in his native land, protesting against a repressive regime. He had championed the works of Dmitri Shostakovich and Sergei Prokofiev when Soviet authorities held them in disfavor. He had not only written an open letter supporting the right of Aleksandr Solzhenitsyn "to write the truth as he sees it" but sheltered the outspoken author and his family in a cottage on his country estate. Solzhenitsyn was living there in 1970 when he won the Nobel Prize for literature. These acts cost Rostropovich his citizenship, cast him into exile, and nearly destroyed his career. But he did them—that is the point.

Once, I was sitting in the office of a man I was interviewing for a business article. His suit jacket was draped over the back of his chair. He was leaning forward, talking enthusiastically about his job, when suddenly his secretary burst into the room.

"He's back. Mr. ______ is back," she said. "He's coming through the door!"

The man blanched. He jumped up and put on his jacket. Small beads of sweat cropped up on his forehead; fear crept into his eyes. He stared at me, obviously hoping I would put on my jacket, too. The conversation continued, but the mood had changed. He sat stiffly. I had to extract information from him a bit at a time. Later, I found out that the man's boss had laid down a rule that all employees were to wear suit jackets while they worked, no excuses, no exceptions, no exemptions.

As I walk the sands of Miramar, I find it easy to pass judgment on events that happened long ago. But I can't help wondering how I would respond if I were caught in that man's trap today. Would I make a fuss? Would I fight back, maybe threaten to quit? Or would I submit to the indignity of my boss's edict and go to work day after day, complying with his miserable rule.

It astounds me when I think of the courage it takes to live, to behave as we want to behave, to be who we want to be. The world is filled with those who would keep us from singing the songs we want to sing, painting the pictures we want to paint, skimming the stones we want to skim. Some are bosses, some are officials of oppressive regimes—and some are our mothers, fathers, teachers, husbands, or wives, who, for whatever their reasons, try to stifle the life force that makes us who we are. But we have this choice: We can empower them or we can empower ourselves.

A few of us seem to know this intuitively from an early age; the rest of us have to learn it through harsh experience. The deep, driving hunger of the soul is there; it will not go away—and we pay an awesome price each time we push it down into the pit of our being. Little by little the colors fade and the sound of music goes out of our lives.

I find myself sitting on a huge boulder by the side of the sea. I don't remember arriving here, but I do know that I automatically park myself on the flat surface of this rock whenever I pass by. As I lean back, words spill out of me into the morning air.

'Twas on the shores that round our coast
From Deal to Ramsgate span,
That I found alone, on a piece of stone,
An elderly naval man. . . .

I first came upon "The Yarn of the Nancy Bell" by the lyricist W. S. Gilbert in the fifth grade, and I was so taken by its swinging rhythm that I committed it to memory—and never forgot it. Through the years it would pop up at odd moments, as it does now, as if to remind me of the music of words:

His hair was weedy, his beard was long,
And weedy and long was he;
And I heard this wight on the shore recite,
In a singular minor key: . . .

I have no doubt that the elderly naval man and I are one and the same, and that we have been brought to this place by a force beyond ourselves to tell stragglers and passersby the tale we have to tell:

O, I am a cook and a captain bold,
And the mate of the Nancy brig,
And a bo'sun tight, and a midshipmite,
And the crew of the captain's gig.

I am reciting loudly and gesticulating wildly, unaware that a woman and a small girl are approaching me from behind. When I see them, I stop. The girl, no more than three, looks up into my face.

"Are you being silly?" she asks.

I have now reached a point in my life where I

regard silliness as a virtue, perhaps the first sign of sanity.

"Yes, I am being silly," I say.

She laughs the contagious laugh of a child. I have that laugh in me. It bubbles up and I laugh, too.

eleven

the surf caster

The wind has shifted to the south and a light mist is blowing in from the sea. There is a desolation to the beach, a sense of desertion, as if the human population has fled to a higher ground in fear of a pending catastrophe. I feel it myself, feel the foreboding, but I don't know where it comes from or what it is.

Down the beach, through the drizzle, I see a solitary fisherman. He is wearing a sou'wester, a yellow slicker, and hip boots pulled up over his jeans. The sight of him evokes a buried image from my past, for I was once a surf fisherman myself, and I stop to chat with him.

He tells me he has already landed nine perch, and he is determined to catch one more before the tide turns. His rig is simple: a slim bamboo rod and a light spinning reel. He casts his sandworm into the breakers, reels in slowly, and suddenly jolts the rod up over his shoulder.

"Got one!" he says.

His rod bends almost to the breaking point; his reel is too light to cope with the fish—if, indeed, that is what is at the other end. It isn't struggling like a bat ray or a striped bass; it seems to be lying under the water, perhaps trapped behind a rock, listless as a cod or a mass of kelp.

The surf caster sticks his rod in a sand spike and begins to pull in the monofilament line, hand over hand, a little at a time. I stare intently at the point where the line enters the sea, hoping that what ultimately emerges is more exciting than a clump of seaweed. Gradually it becomes clear that he has snagged a line, one lost by another angler, who has long since disappeared. His own line comes out first; there is a perch on the hook and a red crab clinging to the wire leader. He switches to the snagged line, dragging hook and sinker up the beach. What we see astounds us both. There is a second perch firmly on the hook, and a mottled cabezon, with spiny fin and gaping mouth, looking for all the world like a prehistoric creature, has seized the smaller prey above the tail and is trying to devour it.

The surf caster kneels on the sand and stares at

his haul with disbelief. With a single cast he has caught three fish and a crab. The crab lets go of the leader, and he lets it crawl back into the ocean. But the two perch and the cabezon he keeps.

"I'm sixty-five," he says to me. "I've been fishing the surf for fifty years, and I've never seen anything like this. Last year I had a heart attack." He thumps his chest. "Too much corned beef and cabbage, steaks and eggs. Now I eat fish, which I catch myself."

Warmed by his exuberance, I continue down the beach. Offshore, a brown pelican plunges headfirst into the ocean. Closer in, a Caspian tern zigzags above the swells. Still closer in, a scoter dives at the last second under the crest of a wave. They are surf fishers all, taking what they need to survive from the sea.

Once, when I worked in Manhattan, I went into Abercrombie & Fitch, the exclusive outfitter to sportsmen, then located on Madison Avenue. On an upper floor, I found the store's fishing expert. "I'm interested in surf fishing," I said. "What do you recommend?"

A tall, imperious man, he drew himself up to full height. "Surf fishing," he replied. "What do you want to do that for? It's the most unproductive kind of fishing there is!" I left and never went back.

I found what I was looking for in a ramshackle

bait and tackle shop located on the pier in the seaside town where I lived. The elderly proprietor picked a fiberglass blank off a wooden rack with his gnarled fingers and held it up for me to inspect.

"This one is nine feet long," he said. "That's all you need. Some fishermen want a rod eleven, twelve, even thirteen feet long. They think they have to cast to England to catch a fish. But all you have to do is reach the breakers. That's where the blues and stripers feed."

He attached cork grips, a seat for the reel, and wrapped the guides. I attached a reel, a leader, and lure, and made a practice cast from the edge of the dock. The rod had exactly the right flex to it—not too limber, not too stiff. It was meant for me.

My career as a surf caster began on the long spit of sand that faces the Atlantic off the south shore of Long Island. Every Saturday morning from September through November, my good friend Bob Behn and I would cross the causeway to the ocean beach, scan the horizon for feeding gulls, and cast our lures into the white water in front of the breakers. Bob, who was my mentor, had a standing rule, and we seldom varied from it.

"Cast three times from one spot," he told me on our very first outing. "If you don't get a strike, walk fifty paces up the beach and cast three more times. Cast and walk, cast and walk. It's the only way."

And that's what we did. Week after week, year after year, Bob and I made our fall pilgrimage to the south-shore fishing grounds. Week after week, year after year, we would cast and walk, cast and walk, from early morning to afternoon. And week after week, year after year, we would go home with no fish.

Yet I cannot say that those long days under the autumn sun were unproductive. Between casts, there were frequent intervals of conversation and reflection that were fruitful beyond belief. Sometimes Bob and I would lean against the lee side of a dune, discussing the stories we had read, the stories we wanted to write. A teacher of English, a lover of literature, Bob had given me an anthology of short fiction, and he would press me for my thoughts.

I must have read a dozen stories in that book, but one in particular remains firmly fixed in my memory. "Old Red," by Caroline Gordon, is a haunting tale of Mister Maury, a freshwater fisherman who, in the eyes of his family, seems to be fly casting his life away. They urge him to do useful work, productive work in the way of the world, but he refuses to change his life, to let them wear him down. Day after day he ventures down to a pond and casts his feathery lures over the placid water with perfect fidelity, hauling in bass and bream.

"What does it mean?" Bob asked. "What do you think it means?"

Although I was moved by the story, I really didn't know. I may have been fishing, but I had no idea why I fished, why Mister Maury fished, why men fished or what they were fishing for.

"Maybe he's just obsessed with fishing," I said. "Maybe that's all the author is trying to say."

"I think Mister Maury fishes," Bob said, "because he has a desire to make his life whole. Fly casting is his art, his craft, his means, his ends, his work, his play. There are no artificial boundaries in his world. He is like the plovers feeding along the shore. They probe, rest, wade, fly; they don't need a vacation to rejuvenate themselves. Their life is of a single piece, and so they are fully alive all the time."

We fished longer than usual that day. It was mid-November, the north wind gusted at our backs, and we knew we wouldn't return to the surf again until the following fall. All through the noon hour, through the early afternoon, we cast our lures into the breakers three times, walked fifty paces up the beach, and cast three times more. With each cast, I thought of Mister Maury and all the fish he took from his tiny pond. And here I was with the wide Atlantic at my feet, and I couldn't catch a thing.

The sun was halfway down the sky when Bob turned to me. "What do you say we call it a day." He removed his lure, put it in his canvas shoulder bag, and snapped the leader to one of the guides.

"Just one more cast," I said.

He laughed. "That's what you always say."

I removed my metal lure and attached a wooden plug. I don't know why I did it; it wasn't skill or intuition. I had no special knowledge that informed me a popping plug would be better at that moment than a shiny lure. I cast high above the churning water and the plug landed with a visible splash. Almost at once I saw a movement, a dark swirl below the plug, and I knew it wasn't an ordinary fish. It struck the plug; I let out a mighty howl and jolted the rod to set the hook.

What followed was sheer panic. Bob was jumping up and down, telling me to keep the rod tilted upward, to tighten the drag, to loosen the drag, to give him more line, to reel him in, to take it easy, to hurry up. Several times I thought I had lost him; then I would reel in furiously until I felt his powerful tug again. Finally, with the help of a wave, I rolled him toward the shore.

"It's a striper," Bob cried. "My God, he's huge!"

When I got him on the beach, he somehow managed to throw the hook. He lay on the wet sand, a yardstick long, flapping furiously. Bob and I stood there staring at the mighty fish, unable to act. We had come all this way for all these days, for all these years, to catch a fish, and now that we had at long last caught one, we didn't have the slightest idea what to do about it. A wave washed up the shore, surrounded the striper, and it swam back into the sea.

"He's gone," Bob said.

"Yes," I said, "he's gone."

We trudged up the beach, our rods over our shoulders, and drove silently home.

That spring Bob accepted a teaching job in the Midwest; by early summer he had moved away. But I went on fishing. I bought short surf rods for my sons, Jeff and Keith, who were of fishing age, and took them to the beach with me as soon as the blues and stripers started to run. I continued to cast lures and poppers, but I let the boys bottom-fish with bait, squid, or sandworms. The luck was with them, for they pulled in fluke, blowfish, and sea robins right away. Long before the season ended, they proclaimed themselves better fishermen than I.

They were then and they are today. But the sea calls to us in different ways.

"The difference between Pop and me," Keith says, "is that I like to catch fish." He plies the Pacific off Southern California and Baja in his small, towable powerboat, an assortment of rods and reels at the ready, depending on what is biting that day. He leaves at dawn, stops at a bait barge, then heads for the oil rigs a dozen miles offshore. If he has no luck there, he tries his other favorite spots—and almost always by early afternoon he has his quota of bonito, sand bass, dorado, or yellowtail.

His freezer is filled with fish. When I visit, he cooks me a magnificent meal over hot coals.

But his assessment is right. His way of fishing is not my way; our reasons for venturing down to the sea are not the same. He is casting for fish, but I am casting for something else. I don't know exactly what it is. It is hidden below the surface, maybe lying on the ocean bottom, an object that I lost a long time ago. It may have been a penknife or an agate shooter or a well-worn baseball mitt.

I have told this story before, and I imagine I shall go on telling it over and over again. My parents died when I was a child, and with their death the avenues to all those who came before me disappeared. I was a man a long time before I found the courage to mourn their passing from my life, and ever since I have been trying to resurrect all the forfeited memories that link me to my past.

My mother's father, Henry Isidore Lewis, was an ardent fisherman. I have a photograph of him, of Izzy, in my family album. He is standing against a backdrop in a photographer's studio, his rod in one hand and a huge striped bass in the other, having his picture taken for posterity. His hat is pulled back jauntily on his head; a tuft of soft white hair slips out under the brim and falls across his forehead. His expression is serious, as if he is saying, *This is how I want the world to remember me.*

Grandpa took me fishing once off a narrow footbridge at Sheepshead Bay; we didn't catch anything. He taught me a fisherman's proverb that day, and it sticks in my mind.

When the wind is from the north,
The fish bite naught.
When the wind is from the east,
The fish bite least.
When the wind is from the south,
The fish bite with the mouth.
When the wind is from the west,
The fish bite the best.

I have never found absolute truth in the saying, but absolute truth is not what I am searching for.

A few years ago, my mother's younger sister, then in her eighties, gave me a copy of Grandpa's death certificate. It showed that he was born in New York City in 1870. I browsed through *The Oxford History of the American People*, searching for a few benchmarks that would help me grasp the full extent of his days. I was astonished to discover that he was born while Ulysses S. Grant was President of the United States, before the first electric streetcar, before the battle at the Little Bighorn. I am saddened to think that all my grandfather's memories died with him, that they have passed into oblivion and can never be recovered. There is something I did not do that I should have done. Had I thought to ask him about his life when he was alive, I could be the one to pass those memories on.

Grandpa had gold coins; he kept them in a desk drawer, and every now and then he would take them out and show them to me. He said his father had been in the gold rush of 1849—that the coins dated back to that time. I don't know what happened to them. They vanished ages ago. Maybe that's what I am surf casting for. Maybe I'm trying to fetch up those old coins.

A few years ago, while traveling through the Scottish Highlands, I took an excursion boat through the Caledonian Canal into Loch Ness. The sky was low and heavy mist blocked my view of the shore. I stood alone on the foredeck, looking across the darkening waters. I could sense the monster of that far northern lake lurking below the surface, exerting a spell that held me in place while the boat slowly circled the frigid body of water in which he dwelled. He did not appear.

Hours later, when the boat pulled into its berth, I was still standing in the same spot. I walked back to town along the banks of the River Ness, resolved to return another day. The following morning I caught an early train to Aberdeen—but the need to see the monster of Loch Ness remained in me. And now I find that the mythical creature is with me still as I walk the sands of Miramar.

The penknife, the agate shooter, the baseball mitt, the gold coins, all have merged in my memory and are now one. All those lost parts of my past life submerged, buried in the deep with the serpent of the lakes and seas. That is what draws me to the edge of the ocean with rod and reel. I cast not for fish but for the leviathan.

Although I have never seen him, I know that the monster possesses no separate identity of his own. He is an aspect of me, a part of my hidden nature, and

I want to pull him up to the surface so I can look at him squarely and make myself whole.

A fine drizzle falls over Miramar, coating my hair. But there is a lightness to my step as I head for the shelter of my beach house a mile away. I will not hurry; I will move so fast and no faster, even if it starts to pour. I feel as if I have shed a burden that had been weighing me down for a long time.

The wind is high and the tide is in. I glance into the breakers; the urge to fish comes over me once more. I want to cast my lure not for the mighty tug but for the nibble at the end of the line. If luck is with me, I might catch a perch or a cabezon.

I remember the nine-foot rod that was made perfectly to suit my purpose so many years ago. If I had it now, I could rig it up and start to cast right away. Then I remember I left it on the other coast with my son Jeff.

When I reach the beach house, I make a long-distance call. Jeff answers. I ask if he still has the rod. "Of course I have it, Pop," he says. "I just used it the other day." He tells me he took his five-year-old son, Trevor, to the same strip of beach Bob and I fished from years before. He hooked a sea robin and Trevor reeled it in. "Now," Jeff says, "he wants me to take him back there every day."

I walk out on my deck and watch the surf, curling high and crashing against the shore. The rain is now coming down hard, soaking my skin, but I don't care. I am aware only of how the past, present, and future are joined. From Grandpa Izzy to grandson Trevor there are five generations, and we are fishermen all.

twelve

written in the sand

The wind comes up out of the southeast, damp and chill. By noon, an hour before the memorial service, the harbor is full. The crowd gathers around the stone monument dedicated to commercial fishermen who have been lost at sea. Now there are four more. They are strangers to me, but their names are indelibly imprinted on the tablet of my mind, as if they were members of my family or my closest friends:

Kirk Pringle, 40
Alex Kovack, 34
Joe Fischer, 53
Les Bronsema, 72

Who are these men—Pringle, Kovack, Fischer, Bronsema—and why should their deaths affect me so? I know nothing about them except what I read in the newspaper or pick up in casual conversation on the pier. They were crab fishermen, I am told, good men, family men, involved in the community.

They went out one morning in two vessels—Pringle and Kovack aboard the *Lisa*, Fischer and Bronsema aboard the *Best Girl*. The red flag was flying high over the harbor; most of the fishermen stayed in port. But these four went to sea. The wind was gusting from the south; the swells were rolling from the north. They got caught in a vortex. Their heavy crab traps shifted from side to side. The boats broke apart and sank.

A bagpiper plays at the far end of the pier, a plaintive sound, like the cry of a killdeer. The families, who left the harbor earlier aboard a fleet of fishing boats, have been strewing flowers on the sea. Now, the private ceremony over, they are returning home. The boats pass through the breakwater, enter the harbor, dock at their berths. The mourners disembark and follow the bagpiper to the stone monument. They take their seats, surrounded by bouquets and floral wreaths. An anchor plaited with petals hangs in front of them, beyond the monument, on a pale blue wall.

The crowd of a hundred or more stands behind them. I stand with them, looking for a familiar face. I don't see anyone I know. A priest appears, uses the monument as a pedestal. He gives a brief eulogy, then intones the names of the lost men. After each name, a young girl strikes a ship's bell, which resonates low and long across the pier.

A local poet sings a fisherman's ballad. A woman who lost a husband and a son to the sea in separate accidents makes a plea for faith in the Savior and everlasting life. Mothers and fathers, wives and daughters, sons and brothers, sisters and friends rise and try to say what words cannot say about their grief. The service ends with "Amazing Grace."

I stroll about the harbor, studying the ships. Somewhere along one of these floating piers there are two empty berths. Where are the *Lisa* and the *Best Girl* now? Where are the men who owned and sailed them, and where are their mates? I am struck by the disparity in their lives. One man dies at thirty-four; another lives to be more than twice his age.

My thoughts go back a half century to my mother's death. I remember the wan face of a woman in a casket, a woman who barely looked like my mother, and I remember how the room in the funeral parlor reeked of perfume. I took a rose from my mother's bier; afterward I placed it between the pages of a Bible. Years later I came upon the pressed flower in the Book of Psalms. I held the stem between my fingers, twisting it slowly, remembering my mother, the kind of woman she was.

When I was little, she taught me how to push saliva under my upper lip and give a Bronx cheer. She touched my toe, my knee, my chest, my head and called me "Toe-knee Chest-nut." She put me on the back of a bike and pedaled up and down the streets of Manhattan Beach, where she grew up, waving and smiling at all the people she knew. Those are the signs of her days, the legacy she left me with.

I threw away the withered rose; it could not bear the weight of all that memory. What I treasured was the image of my mother alive. Now I want to pass that image on, pass it on to my children, pass it on to my children's children, for memory is what I have of the mother who bore me.

But the tragedy of life is that in the inevitable course of history my mother will be forgotten, just as I will be forgotten, just as the four fishermen will be forgotten. For who will take the pains to remember all those who came before me after I am gone? The tragic part of death is not that I die, but that in dying I take with me the last vestige of those who survive in my remembrance of things past.

When I am gone, what will my survivors say? Will they remember my minor deeds, the ones I cherish most? Will they remember that once I sailed a sloop, once I edited a small-town newspaper, once I taught my daughter to read? And what will happen when my survivors die? What will happen to their memory of me?

I once lived in a hilltop house above a cemetery dating back to the 1800s. From time to time I would climb over a low stone wall and wander through the graveyard, examining the weathered and timeworn inscriptions on the headstones of the six people buried there. I would try to piece together the relationship among them, try to figure out what happened to them when they were alive, but the epitaphs were so eroded by the winds of a century that I could barely make out their names.

Who were these strangers who had their final resting place in my front yard? Does anyone remember them now—remember their births, their marriages, the sounds of their voices, the way they walked? They dwelled for a while along the river of life, did their dance, sowed their seeds, and now all that remains of them are bare granite headstones at the bottom of a hill.

They are but six among the untold millions since the dawn of humankind who have come and gone, leaving no trace, no fossil memory of their passage. Kings, emperors, czars, presidents—we have accounts of them in our history books. We know about the bard who wrote *Hamlet*, the musician who composed the *Eroica*, the mathematician who computed the gravitational pull of heavenly bodies. We know their names; we know their works. But, for all their fame, we know little about the sensate life they lived in the flesh day by day—about their hopes for themselves, their ambitions for their children, the daily deeds in which they took the most pride. And of the great mass of ordinary people, we know nothing at all.

A close friend of mine survived a serious heart attack a dozen years ago. After he recovered, I went to see him on his farm in central New York State. A small, vigorous man, he had always lived his life with a keen sense of adventure, never fearful, constantly willing to test, probe, try something new. He had been a high school history teacher for thirty years. When he retired, he bought sixty acres of prime grazing land and, as an experiment, began to breed beefalo, part bison, part cow. In his spare time he painted, played the slide trombone, ran for Congress (he lost by nine votes), and managed a medical clinic for the community.

I was afraid the heart attack might have slowed him down, but, if anything, he seemed more alive after the illness than before. As soon as I arrived, he came bursting out his front door, a pail in each hand. He was wearing the same red peaked cap he always wore to shade his eyes, and his beard, now pure white, was just as bushy as before.

We strolled together along the hedgerows, picking blackberries, eating a few, dropping most into our pails, pausing from time to time to take in the countryside, the silos, the barns, the farmhouses tucked among the rolling hills. We were chatting idly when he suddenly turned to me and said, "What do you think about death?"

I stood with my pail dangling by my side, staring at him for a long time, not sure what to say. I was disconcerted by the question, startled that he raised it at a moment when I had blackberries, and only blackberries, on my mind. I had no desire to discuss death, his or mine, to be reminded that it was there, waiting for us. But he had come face-to-face with death; he knew it might strike him down at any minute, so he could not go on living his life as if it wasn't there.

Sensing my discomfort, he dropped the subject. We went on down the hedgerow, picking blackberries until our pails were full.

But I wish my friend were with me now, in the aftermath of the memorial service for the fishermen, for I have reached a point in my life where I am prepared to answer the question I was so anxious to avoid on that day we picked blackberries on his farm. What do I think about death? I would tell him that it is the constant awareness of death that gives meaning to life. The moment we lose the sense of our own mortality, we succumb to a different kind of death, a death in life, which is a death far worse than the one we fear.

I have a choice, the same choice that faces every man. I can live a frivolous life, trying to impress others with the house I live in, the clothes I wear, the car I drive. I can strive to be a success in the way of the world, seeking the admiration of others, reveling in their jealousy. I can seek domination over my family and fellow workers in a vain attempt to hide my own deficiencies. I can seek fame, which is the most elusive pursuit of all, for it has no substance and soon vanishes in air.

I can indulge in endless prattle about my friends and neighbors, dissipating my life's energy a little at a time. I can wallow in self-pity, refusing to accept responsibility for my own circumstances. I can manipulate others into taking care of me, which is the way of all petty tyrants. I can complain about boredom, as if it were up to those around me to inject excitement into my day.

These are the patterns of the living dead, people who have forsaken life, who are willing to squander their most precious gift, because they refuse to face up to the reality of death. If they wanted to live, truly wanted to live, they would rise up in a resurrection of their own making and commit themselves to the life they have.

"This is the true joy in life," George Bernard Shaw wrote in the dedication to his play *Man and Superman*, "the being used for a purpose recognized by yourself as a mighty one, the being thoroughly worn out before you are thrown on the scrap heap; the being a force of Nature instead of a feverish selfish little clod of ailments and grievances, complaining that the world will not devote itself to making you happy."

I have no way of knowing if the four fishermen were familiar with Shaw's words. But I keep asking myself why they went to sea on that fateful morning instead of waiting for the wind to lighten and the swells to subside. They, along with the other crabbers, had been on strike for three weeks, seeking a higher price for their catch, and the word on the pier is that they were hard-pressed financially. But I am certain that neither they nor their families would have starved if they had bided their time one more day.

I have to believe that it was not money that summoned these fishermen, but an urge, a calling, a passion far more profound. They were a force of nature. Having frittered away three weeks on land, they could no longer resist the mighty purpose of their lives.

I leave the harbor and head home the back way, past the boat launch, past the rocky breakwater, down the sandy shore. The sea is calm. There is barely a ripple on the ocean, but I can hear the wind, and behind the wind I can hear the low blare of a foghorn. It blares again, then again and again. I know that it has been blowing at regular intervals through the morning, as it usually does, but I have only now let it creep into my consciousness.

It occurs to me that the sound of the horn is like the far-off call of death. Occasionally I hear it, but most of the time I push it way down into the base of my being and go about my day as if it wasn't there. But it is there, calling to me in the same way the sea called to those fishermen, and in time it will claim me as it claimed them.

I wonder how much time is left to me. Another minute, another hour, another day? I may collapse before I reach my beach house and take my last breath right here on the sands of Miramar. I may have another lifetime ahead of me; I may live to be twice the age that I am now. I have no way of knowing, and it would not matter if I did. The only thing that matters is that I do not capitulate to fear.

I realize now that I have a task that is greater than all the labors assigned to Hercules. It demands that I live in the richness of this moment because that is all I have or will ever know. It is only when I am fully conscious of the finite nature of my life that I begin to live. The instant I let go of that awareness, I submit to pettiness and drudgery, and the precious seconds slip away.

I look for signs of life; I see them everywhere. High on the bluff above me sits an exotic dwelling hand-built by the photographer who lives there. I stop to admire it, as I have done so many times before. Sometimes it looks like a Norwegian stave church, sometimes like a Shinto shrine, and sometimes like a lapstrake ship plowing through the waves. The bare-breasted figure of a woman, carved in wood, straddles the roof, her arms outstretched, reaching toward the sky.

Farther along I come upon a boy and a girl building what looks like a seaside resort in the sand. They run back and forth to the water's edge, pulling out sea palm and planting the stalks around the perimeter of their structure, with the weedy clumps at the top so that they resemble tropical trees swaying in the breeze.

Beyond the children a bronzed and bedraggled sculptor, bare to the waist, his black hair curling down his neck, is building a driftwood monument to himself out of debris that has floated ashore. He makes use of everything he finds. In the center of his lopsided shelter, a kind of lean-to, sits a stuffed, waterlogged doll in a rope swing. I can hear the sculptor muttering as he works. "Why not! Why not!" he says as he hangs a discarded wading boot with a yellow toe from a rusty nail.

Still farther along the beach, I come upon a mound with a depression in the middle. Two rings surround the mound—an inner one of sea-fig leaves; an outer one of tiny, glistening shells.

There are scribblings, too, still intact in the intertidal zone. Here in the damp sand is an interrupted game of ticktacktoe. *X* could win, or *O* could win, but I don't know whose move it was.

Nearby there is a message: *Happy birthday, Daddy!* in a childish scrawl. Farther down the beach, another message: *Lindsay, are you all right!*

And still farther along: *Pamela was here! Amelia was here! Claudia was here!* Three affirmations, one below the other, encompassed by a heart.

And farther along still, the unsigned testament:

I am here!

I stop and kneel, and below it I write:

I am here, too!

The tide is rising. In a little while the waves will wash my mark away. But right now I am overcome by a need to assert my presence so the world will know I passed this way.

thirteen

by-the-wind sailor

The sky darkens and the wind blows at gale force, driving the sea against the land. When the storm lets up, it leaves the beach littered with transparent blue jellyfish. I see them tumbling in the breakers, floating up the sand, settling by the thousands along the high-water line. They wash ashore for days.

These little jellyfish are called by-the-wind sailors. They have a triangular sail and no rudder, so they can't steer. Unable to set a course of their own, they are blown across the wide Pacific, sometimes this way, sometimes that way, depending on the direction of the wind.

I scoop some up in a clam shell and carry them back to my beach house deck, where I space them out along the top railing and study them for a long time. No bigger than my thumb, they look like tiny plastic toys mass-produced from a common mold. I look across the sea, but I still see them plainly, as if I had painted them on the canvas of my mind. They are sailing aimlessly in great flotillas, going with the breeze.

My thoughts drift to a scorching summer afternoon in the Pocono Mountains. I am with a friend from college days, a man with the most awesome intellect of anyone I have ever known. We are sitting side by side on the edge of a pear-shaped pool outside his hillside home. Every now and then we slip into the water to cool off. Between dips we talk about our mutual desire to separate from our wives.

We attended each other's weddings so many years ago, and each of us believed at the time that our marriages would last forever. Now, more than a quarter century later, we are telling each other that our marriages are faltering, and neither of us knows what to do.

Our conversation is intimate; for a while it feels as if we may be helping each other find the courage we need to act. We talk all through the long afternoon. Exhausted at last, we lapse into silence.

My friend sits with his head bowed, running his stubby fingers through his wavy white hair. He has a bulging forehead, as if there isn't sufficient space inside his skull to hold his brains. I wait patiently for words of wisdom, words that will give me hope. Suddenly he raises his arms in resignation. "But don't you see," he says, "people like you and me don't get divorced."

In the months that followed, I ended my marriage. He remained trapped in his, sinking deeper into anger and despair, caught in the current of social convention, afraid of breaking his vow, afraid of what others might say. For all his brilliance, he could not figure out how to break away. A year after our poolside conversation, he suffered a serious stroke. He lingered awhile, then died.

My thoughts drift further back. I am twelve, in the home of my guardian aunt and uncle, when the doorbell rings. My aunt answers; a neighbor is complaining about gravel that has been dumped in our driveway and has spilled over onto his yard. My aunt is flustered. She reacts as if something dreadful has happened, and that she is to blame.

"I'm sorry," she said. "I will have—" She stops in midsentence, as if she is poised at the edge of a precipice. I wait in the background, wondering what she is about to say. She starts again. "I will have . . . the boy . . . clean it up." The neighbor seems satisfied with that. He turns and walks away.

I go to the garage and grab a shovel. It's not much of a job. In twenty minutes, I have the gravel heaped up where it's supposed to be. But with each shovelful, I hear my aunt's words: "I will have the boy clean it up." The boy is me.

My aunt cooked for me, cleaned for me, put a roof over my head. She did all those things because I was the child of her dead sister, and she saw herself as duty-bound to take me into her home. She went through each day doing her duty to me, demanding my gratitude in return. She never found out that a relationship based on duty is no relationship at all. What she thought about love, affection, consideration, and concern, I cannot say; she never mentioned them. Her sense of duty so overwhelmed her, so deadened her sensibilities, that she could not refer to me as *my nephew, my boy*—could not claim me as her own.

My friend and my aunt were different in virtually every way. Yet they had this one trait in common—they could not alter their course. They worked hard to give the impression that they were steadfast, that they were people who lived up to their obligations. There was a period in my life when I saw them that way. But now they seem to me like rudderless by-the-wind sailors, exercising no control over the direction of their lives.

I go to a bookshelf in my beach house, take down a field guide to the Pacific Coat, and look up *by-the-wind sailor.* It describes a flat, oval skeleton with gas-filled pockets, a large-mouthed feeding tube surrounded by rows of reproductive bodies, and numerous blue tentacles around the rim. I take down another guide and come upon the following definition, written by a marine biologist: "They are variously regarded as colonies of medusa-like individuals called persons. . . ."

The sudden appearance of the word *persons*, with all its human connotations, startles me. I put the guides back on the shelf and return to the edge of the ocean. The *persons* are still tumbling in the breakers, washing up the beach. I settle on the sand and close my eyes. The warmth of the sun seeps into my bones; my mind floats free. I imagine convoys of pale blue shapes drifting across a rimless sea. As they blow with the wind, they are transfigured into people I have known—people who looked as if they knew exactly where they were going.

I did not realize this when I was younger, but I do now. Those individuals who seem most resolute, who seem so sure of themselves, are often the ones who have lost their way. They rush about, expending enormous amounts of energy presenting a picture of themselves to the world, a picture they want us to believe; but after a while the picture wears thin and we see through to the frightened soul inside.

We come upon them everywhere, masters of self-deception, deceiving others even as they deceive themselves. Most are ordinary people; they live in the house across the street or work in the office down the hall. Because they convey an aura of self-assurance, an air of certainty, some rise to exalted positions.

They rule from the executive suite; they exhort from the pulpit; they strut around the football field. Here are the robber barons who build their fortunes on watered stock and junk bonds. Here are the bombastic preachers who prey on the blind faith of their followers. Here are the honored athletes who batter women.

For a while they lead us astray. They loom as heroes, as gods; we invest them with magical powers to make up for the defects we see in ourselves. Then one day we find out that for all our frailties, for all our faults, for all our flaws, they are the weak and we are the strong.

Here on the sands of Miramar, so far from the fields where people vie for wealth and power, there is one thing I can afford to admit to myself that I never could before. I am confused; I do not have an answer to every question that comes my way.

In the past, I viewed this lack of certainty in myself as a sign of weakness. I yearned for an absolute truth, an ideology, something that would cover every contingency in my life, tell me what to think and how to behave. Searching, I read great poets and philosophers—Lao-tzu, Thoreau, Tolstoy, Whitman, Shaw. I gathered them in with all their inconsistencies, paradoxes, and disharmonies. I discovered that each had a piece of the truth for me, and that in moments of need I could pick and choose. "Do I contradict myself?" Walt Whitman wrote. "Very well then I contradict myself, (I am large, I contain multitudes)."

Now I see that to be confused is to be strong. Confusion forces me to assess my situation, to move with care, to evaluate my progress and correct my course as I go along. There is no dogma, no ideology, no absolute truth for me to fall back on. It took me the better part of a lifetime to come to terms with that. But once I did, it set me free to explore the world and find out for myself what I believe.

I come upon men and women suffering from dogma sickness all the time. The symptoms are there, in the tone of their voice, the purse of their lips, the furrow of their brow. I would like to tell them how liberated, how exhilarated they would feel if only they could find the courage to let go. But I know that no matter what I say they will go on clinging to their creed with all their might because they are too afraid to face the randomness of life and make decisions on their own.

Only the weak believe they possess answers to all the questions; only the weak mount the public stage swelled with swagger, filled with cant. Only the weak tell others what to think and how to act, based on their ideology. Only the weak aspire to be demagogues.

Hitler claimed he had the absolute truth. So did Mussolini, so did Stalin. They were the terrors of my youth, men with the blood of millions on their hands. To kill, to murder, to slaughter—that was as nothing to these despots because they held to an absolute truth, which, in their distorted view, sanctified their deeds.

In the United States, we have been lucky; in our moments of peril, when it sometimes seemed as if the nation might not survive, genuine leaders have emerged as if from the soil with a true sense of wit and proportion. I think of those who were great: Thomas Jefferson, Abraham Lincoln, Franklin Roosevelt. They were not ideologues, not conservatives or liberals, not captalists or socialists, not hawks or doves. They were pragmatic men seeking commonsense solutions to the pressing problems of their day: tyranny, slavery, the preservation of the union, the Great Depression, worldwide war.

They were not always consistent in their public or their private lives. They could be devious, even calculating, when they believed they needed to be. They were highly political, waiting for the favorable moment to speak, the propitious moment to act. I accept all these traits as signs of their humanity. I admire these men because they were driven not by the winds of ideology but by something deeper, something more profound. It was their compassion—not their creed, not their doctrine, not their dogma—that changed the world.

I yearn for leaders who are not addicted to any party or any creed. Instead, I get zealots, some religious, some political, who rise up on public platforms, command the airwaves, and announce that they have the solution to all the problems that plague mankind. Perhaps that is the purpose, the only purpose, of the doctrines they espouse—self-aggrandizement. They concoct a web of conceit to call attention to themselves.

The struggle is not for power, not for wealth, not for fame. The struggle is for authenticity. The struggle is to live without guile, without artifice, without chicanery, so that we may become the men or the women we were born to be. I say this now as if the thought began with me, but I borrowed it from Polonius, who spoke it long before I came along:

This above all: to thine own self be true,
And it must follow, as the night the day,
Thou canst not then be false to any man.

Polonius is supposed to be a sententious old fool, and that is how he is almost always played. But that is merely Shakespeare's ruse, his test for the playgoer, you and me. He assigns his words of wisdom not to kings and princes, but to clowns, jesters, and buffoons.

There are those who view this sojourn of mine along the sands of Miramar as aberrant behavior, a way of escaping the pressures of the world. A friend inquires in a recent letter if it isn't time to stop "this idleness, this drifting. When will it all end? Where will it all lead?" he wants to know. I send him a postcard, thanking him for his concern, assuring him that I am well. I do not address his question, but the answer burns in my brain: It will lead where it will lead. It will end when it will end.

Alone on the beach, gazing into the breakers, I am more sure of my destination than ever before. I am not drifting. I am moving by design, aware of the teeming life about me and the choices I must make—when to resist, when to accept, when to bide my time.

Those who ignore the words of Polonius, who are not true to their nature, who are driven by forces beyond themselves, they are the drifters of the world. When the wind shifts, so must they.

I rise and continue for a mile, two miles, three miles, wading in the surf, the jellyfish brushing against my legs, washing over my feet. It seems to me there are more by-the-wind sailors on my stretch of beach than people in the world. Hapless, they collect in long, winding ridges on the sand, where they wither and die.

fourteen

the sphinx of the seashore

I keep thinking of Paul Gauguin. As I sit on the beach reading his journals, I discover that his journey to paradise was not much different from mine to Miramar. As a young man, he got distracted and for a while he lost his way.

Gauguin was only twenty-three when a friend of his family secured a position for him in a stock-broking firm. He was only twenty-five when he married Mette Sophie Gad, a prim and prudish Danish woman. They had five children in ten years, and he loved them. But it was the wrong job and the wrong woman at the wrong time.

When he was thirty-one, he painted *Mette Sewing*, a cozy domestic portrait. She is sitting at a table, her figure covered by a loose dress. Only her face and hands are bare. About the same time he painted the nude study *Suzanne Sewing*. The full-bodied woman in the painting, a professional model, is sitting on cool white sheets at the edge of a bed, mending what appears to be a gauzy undergarment. A shapely mandolin hangs in the background, suspended from a purple wall, adding a seductive note. A critic referred to Suzanne as "a woman of our day." Mette so despised the painting that she refused to give it houseroom.

His business career did not go well. He and Mette moved from Paris to Rouen and then to her native Denmark. He went from stockbroking to banking to selling tarpaulins. But the desire to paint was there, as it was from the beginning, and it could not be suppressed. Agitated and despondent, caught between art and commerce, he went on painting because that was the only life he knew.

The popular notion is that one fine day he suddenly left for Papeete, going from businessman to artist, forsaking wife and children in an impulsive leap. But his route to the lush tropical isles of Oceania was far more roundabout. He went from Denmark to Paris, to Brittany, to Martinique, then back to Paris and Brittany. He was in his early forties when at long last he reached Tahiti, the one place on earth where he felt at home.

There, in the fragrant land, he painted as he wished to paint, in jungle colors, parrot colors, in violets, somber blues, vermilions, orange-tinted yellows, and rich golds. He painted the landscape, the women of the landscape, still and statuesque, unsullied by European civilization, dwelling in a luxuriant realm somewhere between the actual and the spirit world. He painted in poverty, in sickness, in fever. He did not drive himself to paint, any more than he drove himself to breathe. He painted because not to paint was unthinkable.

In 1891, shortly after his arrival, he painted *Vahine No Te Tiare* (*Woman with a Flower in Her Hair*), one of his first portraits of a native woman. It is unforgettable: the dark, handsome head against a brilliant yellow background, a barely visible white flower in her straight black hair. She is wearing a deep blue dress with white cuffs and collar, set against a disk of sunset red. Green leaves and white flowers flutter like butterflies about her noble head, and she holds a green sprig ever so tenderly between the curled fingers of her hand.

He wrote about *Vahine No Te Tiare* in *Noa Noa*, his account of his first two years in paradise:

> I worked quickly—with a passion. It was a portrait which was true to what my eyes veiled by my heart truly perceived. I believe that above

> all else it revealed what went on inside her; the strong flame of a restrained force. She had a flower in her ear which absorbed her own perfume. Her face, in its majesty, and with its raised cheekbones, reminded me of a phrase from Poe: "No beauty is perfect without a certain singularity in its proportion."

She is a foretelling of Tehamana, maybe Tehamana herself, the woman of the island who gave herself to Gauguin as artist and man, lifting him out of his despair so he might do the work he was meant to do. She asked nothing of him, expected nothing from him. She was there, always there, when he was working, when he was dreaming, waiting in silence, knowing when to speak, when not to speak, filling the thatched hut in which they dwelt with her perfume.

On the other side of the world, Mette waited, too. Consumed with bitterness, she criticized the paintings he sent her, sold them without comprehending them, and demanded, constantly demanded, that he send her money he didn't have. In the eyes of her friends and family, she was justified, for he had Tahiti, but she had the care and feeding of their children.

In 1893, he returned to France for an exhibition of his work, but the lure of the South Seas was too powerful to resist. By 1895, he was back in paradise, this time for good. But there was a residue of guilt, and it preyed on him. He wrote to a friend:

> Look what I have done with my family life; I ran away without any warning, letting my family solve its problems by itself, for I am the only person who could help it any way. But I am really going to finish my life here, and, as far as I am concerned, in complete tranquility. Of course, this means I am an utter scoundrel. But what does it matter? Michelangelo was too, and I'm not Michelangelo. . . .

In August 1897, he wrote to Mette:

> Madame, I asked you that on 7 June, my birthday, the children should write "Dear Papa" to me with a signature. You replied, "You have no money, don't count on it."
>
> I shall not say, "God guard you," but more realistically, "May your conscience sleep to save you waiting for death as a deliverance."

His final words to her, a hammer blow.

I sit upright on the sand, the journal in my lap, remembering how I felt when my children were small. I was a newspaperman, living on a reporter's meager salary, but I yearned for a home for myself and my growing family. A real estate agent showed me every house in my price range; I rejected them all. Then one afternoon she drove down a tree-lined street in an exclusive part of town and parked in front of a white Dutch Colonial. The house had a long center hall, a formal dining room, a living room with a brick fireplace and French doors at either end that opened onto a porch, an oak-paneled family room, a staircase that led to a landing with a window seat, then turned up to the second floor.

Before marriage, I had thought of myself as one who would starve in an artist's garret before succumbing to the creature comforts of a white house with blue shutters set so properly on a green lawn. I had a small inheritance, which I used as a down payment. My family and I lived in that Dutch Colonial for twelve years. But the artist hunger remained, simmering under the surface, burning in the soul. After a while I felt as if I were an imposter, a man pretending to be at home in a house he no longer wanted to own.

Is that how Gauguin felt when he made the missteps of a young man? There is a formal portrait of Paul and Mette, a photograph taken in Copenhagen in the twelfth year of their marriage. Mette, wearing a long dress and light jacket with a collar fitting snugly around her neck, is sitting stiffly in a curved chair with a tassel dangling from its back. Paul is standing behind her, body aslant, legs crossed, left hand on his hip, right hand braced against a stack of books on a tabletop. Who was the artist deceiving when he posed for that masquerade?

Gauguin had less than twenty years of life left in him when that photograph was taken. Even then, in his darkest moments, in his secret thoughts, he must have known what riches he would leave behind. He must have known that the further he strayed from himself, the more arduous the journey home. But whatever the price, the journey had to be made; it had to be made.

My thoughts are broken by a horse kicking up sand, which blows in my face as he gallops by, no more than twenty-five feet away. Horse and rider arrive so suddenly, pass by so swiftly, they take my breath away. I watch as they fly down the beach and disappear in the haze. A sign on the beach, duly posted by authorities, prohibits horseback riding, but I see horses and riders along the beach almost every day.

I head down the beach in the direction of the horse and rider; all at once they emerge as one from the mist and pass me again, going the other way. I admire the animal, his power and gait, and I admire the grace of the rider high up on the saddle, so perfectly poised. Behind me, a siren wails.

I turn to see a four-wheel-drive vehicle driven by a park ranger roaring up the beach at top speed, leaving deep tracks in the sand. The race is on. The ranger is chasing horse and rider, and horse and rider are fleeing as fast as they can. I imagine the high-horsepower car overtakes the low-horsepower horse somewhere in the fog that is blowing in from the sea.

I continue the opposite way, considering my options, the speed at which I choose to move through the world. Walking the beach, I progress at a human pace, two, three, perhaps four miles per hour. Mounted, I gallop at twenty miles per hour, but I leave the human dimension and enter horse time. In a car, I shift to combustion-engine time, which is the artificial clock—days compressed into hours, hours into minutes, minutes into seconds—that I am forced to live by whenever I leave Miramar.

Often, when I am driving, a car will pull out of a side street, barely braking for a stop sign. The driver will have gained ten seconds on his route to somewhere, or so he thinks. But he is traveling at an inhuman rate of speed, so he has no way of knowing how much life he loses in the time he thinks he saves.

We live in an age of hysteria. In a frenzied period of my existence, I once flew through two time zones in the morning, and in the evening flew back through the same two time zones again. I passed myself coming and going. For days afterward I was dazed and disoriented, but I walked around as if I were sane and the flights made sense. It never occurred to me how completely the thrust of the jet engine dictated the terms of my daily life.

Of all the earthbound animals, only man elects to travel faster than his legs can move. It is speed that takes us away from the journey to the center of ourselves. It seems to me that the faster we go, the more jaded we become. The boredom mounts; we respond with still more speed. At sixty miles per hour, we lose all sense of where we are going and who we are. We step down harder on the pedal, hoping to find the missing person somewhere down the road. At seventy, eighty, ninety miles per hour, we plunge headlong over a precipice and kill ourselves.

How many appointments can we keep in a single day? How many sights and sounds can we absorb before we go completely out of our minds? We admire motion, abhor stillness, treat the reflective person with disdain. I don't have time to sit around contemplating my navel, the man of action likes to say, never thinking that the umbilicus is the center of his being, the point of nourishment that connects him to his future and his past.

Paul Gauguin escaped to the South Seas. A few close friends understood; everyone else considered him eccentric, an intransigent painter of orange rivers and red dogs. But he was engaged in a pilgrimage of a particular kind. "In order to produce something new," he said to a critic, "you have to return to the original source, to the childhood of mankind."

The "something new" he had to produce was himself, his authentic self, the same task that taxes the artist in us all. Wracked by illness, tormented by poverty, plagued by the death of his daughter, he began the one painting above all others he deemed his masterwork. In February 1898, he wrote to a friend, "I have decided before I die to paint a great picture, which is in my head, and all this month I have worked on it in a kind of unaccustomed frenzy."

He called the painting *Where have we come from? What are we? Where are we going?* It is an allegory, primitive, deliberately devoid of perspective. At the lower right, a baby sleeps peacefully beside three women in the shade of a tropical tree; at the lower left, an old woman sits, her head in her hands, resigned. Between them there are other figures: a child eating fruit, a woman picking fruit, another woman listening intently to a goddess standing on a stone pedestal. "The idol," Gauguin wrote, "its two arms rhythmically and mysteriously raised, appears to indicate the hereafter."

The nude figures in the foreground stand out in bright orange. But the scene, oceanic and idyllic, is set beside a stream with the sea and then the mountains of a neighboring island in the background. "Despite certain tonal passages, the general aspect of the work from one end to the other is blue-green, like Veronese," according to the creator of this strange, compelling masterpiece.

Peopled as it is with the symbols of his Tahitian life, the painting confounded viewers in the civilized world, who stared at it in disbelief. What is the meaning of the white bird, the blue idol, the purple shegoat? Why is the orange nude sitting with her back turned, her hand arching over her head? Who are the two women in a leafy bower, cloaked in purple, and what are they talking about?

At another moment in my life, I might have asked myself the same questions. Now I dismiss the symbols of Gauguin's idyll as the least-important aspect of his work. For me, the power of the painting lies not in what it signifies but in what it is. The work bespeaks an inner harmony that belies the anguish of the painter's life.

After he finished the work, he went into the mountains and swallowed arsenic, but the dosage was too small and he survived. His final eight years in the South Seas were the most productive of his life: one hundred paintings, four hundred woodcuts, twenty sculptures and wood carvings. He died in May 1903, a pauper, deeply in debt, never knowing how much the world owed him.

I look about me; the shore, the dunes, the bluffs are transformed into planes of color, a seascape defined by delicate gradations and subtle hues. Boundaries disappear; I am drawn into the painting, too. The pain-filled life of the artist Paul Gauguin passes into myth, like the pagan gods of Mount Olympus, like Prometheus, Sisyphus, Icarus, like Odysseus and his fateful voyage back to Ithaca and home.

I return to my beach house, a deep longing somewhere within me. I have been beachcombing for months, collecting bits of shell and pieces of stone. Now I have a desire to go beyond the bounds of Miramar. I drive into the city, to the museum in Golden Gate Park, and wander through the galleries, searching for Gauguin. I can't find him anywhere, but in a corner of a quiet room, I come upon an oil on canvas by Elihu Vedder, called *The Sphinx of the Seashore*.

In the background, ruins appear: Roman

arches, bleached bones, conch shells, the broken hull of a ship, a half-buried anchor chain. The sky is low and ominous with a reddish glow from the sunset filtering through a cover of cumulus clouds.

In the foreground, the sphinx stretches across the sand, not a stone monument, but a living creature with a woman's head and breasts and a feline lower body and tail. Her long red hair falls in bangs over her forehead; she has an anguished expression on her face. Part human, part cat, she sprawls on the beach, lips apart, eyes wide and filled with expectation, holding me in her gaze.

As I stand staring, I remember the story of Oedipus' journey. In search of his origins, he travels from Corinth to Thebes, but when he reaches the gates of the ancient city, he finds his way blocked by the Sphinx, who holds the inhabitants hostage, killing those who fail to answer her riddle:

What goes on four feet, on two feet, and three
But the more feet it goes on, the weaker it be?

Oedipus answers: Man—who as an infant crawls on all fours, as an adult walks on two feet, and in old age moves with the help of a cane. The Sphinx, distraught that Oedipus has solved the riddle, kills herself, and Thebes is saved.

I leave the museum, the riddle still running through my mind. I lean against a parapet and look out at the city, at the red glow reflecting off the surrounding hills as the sun goes down. The city is modern, as modern as any city can be, but I am confronted with the same life-and-death sentence as a citizen of Thebes.

The riddle of the Sphinx is the riddle of man, and the question posed by the Sphinx comes from ourselves. It is the question Gauguin asked when he painted his masterpiece; it is the question that underlies all questions, and if I ask it honestly, the answer will come to me honestly, as in a prayer.

There is so much I want to do, so much I want to achieve. I want to read the works of Dostoyevsky; I want to sail the fjords of Puget Sound; I want to find a woman who brings me joy. This evening the sun sets at 7:43, tomorrow at 7:41. The days grow shorter. There is so much living to do, and so little time.

Once I was an infant; now I am an adult; soon I will be an old man. Is that how my life goes, in giant leaps from one state of existence to another, without awareness of what I am experiencing now? There was a period when I viewed my life as an inexorable progression of days, but I realize that was a waste, a way of obliterating time.

My life is a speculation, like a work of art. I

begin with a simple brush stroke, not knowing where it will lead. I follow my guesses, my hunches, my instincts; little by little a portrait of myself appears. It takes a lifetime to complete the painting, but I keep at it, arranging and rearranging the parts, filling in the forms, shapes, colors, a brush stroke at a time.

Gradually, if I go with courage and wisdom, I arrive at my destination, a place called paradise. It is not a land free of struggle, a realm devoid of pain or grief. But it is the place where I feel at home, where I am supposed to be.

I drive back to my beach house in twilight. By the time I arrive, the sun has fallen below the horizon and the moon is climbing the sky. I sit on my deck, watching its flight, the riddle of the Sphinx still occupying my mind. Oedipus gave his answer and delivered Thebes; I give my answer and deliver only myself. But I am content, for I saved one man this day.

fifteen

woman fishing from a pier

The women, the women, they are everywhere, stretched in the sun, sitting on the sand, wading in the sea. But nowhere do I see the woman I am looking for.

I walk up a ramp that leads to the pier. I go into a dockside restaurant and order a bowl of red chowder and a glass of wine. I leave the restaurant and stroll down the pier.

At the end of the pier a barefoot woman fishes. Her hair, black and plaited, hangs halfway down her back in a single braid. She is wearing faded jeans and a gauzy powder blue blouse, which clings to her body from the wind and spray. The sleeves are pushed up, revealing bronzed forearms. She casts over a railing and reels in slowly, shrewdly, as if she knows what lurks on the ocean floor.

I look in the pail beside her, trying to count her

catch. She sees me there, but she does not speak. After a while her rod bends. She sets the hook, reels in a ling-cod, and drops it in the pail.

"How many is that?" I ask.

"Eight," she says. "Five rock fish, three cod."

She goes back to casting with the same naturalness as before. I ask about her rod, her reel, her bait, her line. She answers simply, telling me what I want to know.

"You're good at this," I say.

"I ought to be," she replies. "I've been doing it since I was a girl."

She begins to talk, not hesitatingly, as if we are strangers, but openly and easily, as if there are certain things about her I ought to know. She tells me that her name is Anna, that she is Portuguese, that she has lived here, by the sea, all her life. Her hoarse voice seems to rise from a secret place in her chest, and her words spill out with conviction and pride.

She fishes and talks at the same time, sometimes glancing back over her shoulder at me, sometimes over the water at her line. When she finishes, I tell her about myself—who I am, where I live, why I have come to Miramar. Since my arrival, I have guarded myself against the encroachment of others, but standing here on the pier, talking with a woman I never saw before, the barriers fall away and the conversation flows.

After a while I realize that a long time has passed since she had a nibble.

"The fish seem to have gone somewhere else," I say.

"Yes," she replies. "The tide is ebbing now."

I watch her remove hook and sinker and snap her leader to a guide. She picks up her pail, looks across the water one last time, then turns to me.

"Do you know the Chamarita?"

"The Chamarita? No. What is it?"

"I will take you to the Chamarita," she said. "Then you will understand."

I stand on the pier, looking after her, the husky lilt of her voice rising through the empty space of my life long after she disappears.

When I reach my beach house, I take a magazine from a top desk drawer. I have carried this magazine with me for years. I open it to an earmarked page and look for perhaps the thousandth time at the photograph of a woman in a semisheer shirtwaist dress fishing from a pier. She is standing barefoot, with a surf rod in her hands, casting into the sea. Although I never put her picture on display, she is my pinup girl.

I think of Anna at the moment I saw her, standing at the end of the dock in her powder blue blouse, casting her baited line. Was she all she appeared to be, or merely a product of my imagination conjured up out of my longing and need? *I will take you to the Chamarita. Then you will understand.*

The air is crystalline as Anna and I head down the beach toward the heart of town. She is wearing a white shirt and a purple skirt that billows softly in the morning breeze. Overhead the gulls are fluttering through the sky. Anna chants, "*Chama Rita! Chama Rosa! Qué bonita! Qué formosa!*"

She tells me the Chamarita is the traditional song and folk dance of the Portuguese. Today the Chamarita and the Festival of the Holy Ghost are joined. "This is our Thanksgiving," she says, "our way of expressing our thanks for the blessing the people of the Azores received five hundred years ago."

She tells me that in the fifteenth century a volcano erupted on the islands, causing famine and drought. The people came together and prayed, asking the Holy Ghost for help. On the morning of Pentecost there was a great rising sun, and in the sunrise the people of the Azores saw a ship laden with food coming into port.

When Queen Isabel heard of this providence, she ordered a solemn procession in honor of the Holy

Ghost. Accompanied by her maids, she carried her crown through the streets of Lisbon to a cathedral, where she left it on the altar as an offering of thanks. The people of the Azores vowed that they, their children, and their children's children would celebrate Pentecost by expressing their thanks to Queen Isabel for the sacrifice she made.

Anna and I enter the town. The streets have been closed to traffic. The people are already present in large numbers, sitting on the curbs, standing on the corners, the children spilling into the streets. Everyone knows Anna, and Anna knows everyone: the mechanic and his children, the waitress and her fiancé, the beautician and her husband, the bank teller and his wife. She finds a place to watch, an opening in the crowd across from Our Lady of the Pillar, where the parade will end.

The procession moves slowly, fraught with symbols, filled with surprise, totally unformed. A fife and drum corps files past playing the song "Tradition" from *Fiddler on the Roof*, the musical about Jewish life in czarist Russia. The players are wearing red jackets, white pants, and broad-brimmed military hats with red and white plumes.

There are bands from Miramar, Pescadero, San Gregorio, Santa Cruz, and San Jose, girls in white capes, mothers in flowered dresses, old men in suits of gray. A boatload of bread goes by, flanked by boys in white shirts and red scarfs. Another boy holding a diaphanous parasol escorts a little girl in a white gown. The girl supports a pillow in front of her on her arms, and on the pillow sits a dove.

Three teenage girls appear, walking slowly along the route of the parade. The one in the middle, framed by a rectangular garland of flowers, carries a silver crown. She wears a white dress and a dark blue cape that trails behind her along the macadam road. When she reaches the church, the procession dissolves. Anna takes my arm. We mingle with the swirling throng. All about me, people are speaking Portuguese. The men are upright, the women direct.

We enter the church together to witness the blessing of the crown. A priest reads from the Gospel According to John. I am drawn to the stained-glass portraits in the windows, illuminated by shafts of light: Santa Barbara, San Fernando, San Antonio, Santa Ines, San Diego, San Buenaventura, San Luis Rey. The worshipers, of many faiths, sing "Come Holy Ghost" and "Amazing Grace."

As we leave the church, a small girl runs up to Anna, throws her arms around her neck, gives her a hug, and runs off again.

"That is my niece," Anna says. "One day she will be the queen and carry the crown."

"Were you ever the queen?" I ask.

"Yes, I was the queen."

I will take you to the Chamarita. Then you will understand. She belongs to this place; she is part of it and it is part of her. But she is herself, her distinct self, too. She has her own way of listening, her own way of speaking, her own way of blending her present with her past. She is at one with herself, at peace with all the aspects of her life.

The crowd disbands; the traffic starts to flow again. We wander through the streets of the town. Anna touches my hand and points to the coastal range, lush from spring rains; it rises to the north and east, sloping upward at the end of every avenue. It is a wordless gesture, eloquent for its simplicity, but I know at once what she means to say and how she feels, because I feel that way, too.

A fragrance, light as the breeze, sifts through the air. We stroll through the flower market, the sidewalk awash with color, as if Pierre-Auguste Renoir himself had come to town and painted the scene. Men, women, children wander under the canopied booths, make their purchases, and carry off their bouquets. Anna points to the flowers and says their names as we pass by: baby's breath, anemone, larkspur, yarrow. I buy a yellow tea rose and she puts it in her hair.

Across from the flower market there is an alley; halfway down the alley, a vintage clothing shop. We pause, look in a window, and step inside. The shop is small, barely big enough to move around in. The merchandise is stacked on counters and tabletops. In front of me lies a black velvet evening bag lined with ivory satin and lace. I pick it up and finger its rhinestone clasp. It looks like something my grandmother might have carried with her to a formal dance—if my grandmother had ever gone to a formal dance. I fish around inside and pull out a collapsible tortoiseshell comb with a narrow, oddly shaped handle at one end.

Anna takes the object from the palm of my hand and flips it open. "Women would comb their hair like so," she says, "then use the rat-tail end to make a curl." She tries to show me, but her hair is too tightly bound. She hands the comb back to me.

"Do you like it?" she asks.

I drop the comb in the bag and put the bag back on the table.

"No," I reply. "I don't like evening bags, and I don't like curls."

"Do you know what you like?"

"Yes, I know what I like."

"And what do you like?"

I turn slowly, letting my eyes roam the room. A straight chair stands in a corner, with a triangular mass of material draped over the back. It is black—black as her hair. I run my hand across its filigreed border and through its long, silky fringe.

"I like this," I say.

"Do you? It's a fine wool shawl, and it's very old."

She lifts it from the chair and arranges it over one shoulder, then over both shoulders, then over her head and shoulders. She flips the loose ends over her arms. Finished, she folds it neatly and puts it back on the chair.

"And I like this," I say, picking up a straw hat with a broad brim. She puts on the hat, tilting the brim first to one side, then the other, and finally turning the brim up and back off her face. It is dark in the shop, but I can imagine the hat with sunlight filtering through the swirls of woven straw.

"If I could paint," I say, "I would paint you in that hat."

"I will paint you in it," she says. Before I can reply, she goes to the register, buys the hat, and hands it to me. It fits perfectly.

We leave the shop and meander through the streets of the town, returning home the way we came, walking slowly along the beach, pausing from time to time to share a thought.

Later, alone in the gathering darkness, I ponder a question that has been haunting me. Why didn't I meet Anna ages ago, when I was young? I didn't meet her because I didn't see her, even though I probably passed her, or someone like her, many times without ever knowing she was there. Like an infant just out of its mother's womb, my eyes were not yet fully opened.

After all these reflective days combing the sands of Miramar, I understand that we see only what we are ready to see when we are ready to see it. There is a perpetual dawn rising within us. If we are awake to it, it continues to rise gradually, imperceptibly, throughout our lives. With each passing day we shake the sleep from our eyes.

I came to Miramar seeking an end to my isolation and my loneliness. But before I could find Anna, I had to discover myself. I had to locate the swift, sure current that courses through my life and stay with it straight through to the end. Once I found the courage to do that, the woman I was looking for appeared, not as apparition but as flesh and blood, right before my eyes.

I go to bed early and sleep deeply. In my dreams, I am at the Chamarita. Anna is with me, and we are standing side by side, watching the parade. All through the night, I wake and dream, wake and dream, and the dream is always the same. I am at the Chamarita with Anna, watching the boy with his parasol, the girl with her dove, the queen with her crown. Awake, the dream remains: Anna and I standing together on the edge of the sidewalk, two separate people sharing the same space at the same precious moment in time.

In the morning, I go out on my deck and sit, content to do nothing. It is late in the afternoon when I see a patch of washed-out purple far down the shore. Anna is strolling along the water's edge, one hand holding a canvas bag, the other lifting her skirt as the waves wash over her legs. When she reaches a point below the beach house, her head disappears behind a dune, then bobs up again at the bottom of the deck. She climbs the stairs. When she reaches the top rung, she puts down her bag and looks at me.

"So," she says, "are you ready?"

I nod.

She positions a rattan chair at the far end of the deck and slumps into it at an angle to the sea.

"Sit here," she says, "like so."

I sit as she says, my arms folded across my chest. She unlocks my arms; they fall loosely onto my lap. She picks up the straw hat and fixes it on my head. I reach up to help and she lightly slaps my hand.

"Don't touch," she says.

She keeps urging me to hold still, but she doesn't seem to mind if my eyes roam. I shift my gaze from Anna, sitting in a chair with a drawing board on her lap, to the beach, then back to Anna again. What she doesn't know is that while she is painting me, I am painting her.

How is it, how is it, I wonder, that love can come this way? It is a blessing that falls of a sudden, like rain out of a summer sky. One moment I am walking a lonely stretch of beach; the next I am talking to a woman fishing from a pier. She invites me to the Chamarita. I buy her a flower; she buys me a hat. Now she is on my deck, looking at me carefully, her head tilted, her lips pursed, a pastel crayon poised between the fingers of her hand.

It is late when she finishes. The sun has dropped behind the evening clouds. Flashes of burnt crimson fill the sky. I rise from my chair and move toward her cautiously, afraid of what I might find. She lifts the drawing board from her lap, turns it, and shows it to me. I am amazed at what I see. She has painted me in my own image.

sixteen

the beachcomber of miramar

Quietly, without fanfare, a sculptor has come to Miramar. I see his handiwork, one stone heaped upon another along the rocky shore. Now, for the first time, I come upon the artist himself, a slim, slightly stooped man with thick tinted glasses, a red bandanna wrapped around his head. Absorbed in his task, he moves easily, methodically, amid the riprap dumped beside a seawall, carefully selecting boulders and stacking them so they resemble human forms.

I watch him rearrange rock and rubble, transforming the chaos along this stretch of coast into a sculpture garden. He lifts an oblong chunk of concrete and lugs it twenty feet to an open area, places a sloping concave rock on top of it, and a rounded smaller rock on top of that. Three rocks chosen at random, that's how they appear to me. But the sculptor sees them in the aggregate. Assembled, they become a woman in an ankle-length, deeply pleated skirt carrying a bread basket in her outstretched arms.

The female figure, so perfectly proportioned, has the seductive grace and charm of ancient Buddhist idols I have often admired in museums. I approach it cautiously, afraid that if I get too close it will tumble down. I want to touch it, but the structure seems so precarious that I don't dare.

The sculptor, who has ignored my presence until now, turns toward me. "Blow on it!" he says.

I take a deep breath and blow as hard as I can several times on all sides. The sculpture withstands the blasts of air from my lungs.

"If it doesn't fall over when you blow on it," he says, "then the chances are good that only the incoming tide or a strong wind will knock it down."

"And when that happens?" I ask.

"When that happens, I come back another day and set it up again."

Gently, I touch the structure; its stability surprises me. It seems to be defying gravity. I ask the sculptor if he notches the rocks, applies an adhesive, or joins them with a hidden wire. He empties his pockets to prove that he uses no tools, employs no artifice beyond the intuition lodged in his dexterous fingers and roving eyes.

"How do you do it?" I ask. "How do you balance them this way?"

He goes about his work, inspecting rocks, turning them over, moving them about. I wait, wondering if he is going to respond. After a while he says, "I don't think. I just pick up rocks and put them on top of each other."

Despite his reticence, I manage to pull information from him. He tells me that he works on a flower farm farther down the coast, and that he erects sculptures on the beach in his spare time. I press him, try to find out why he is drawn to these rocks, why he feels compelled to transfigure them into human shapes and forms. There is no money in it, no glory, no enduring fame. He does not gloat over his creations; he does not pander to the whims of admirers like me. He shrugs and goes on stacking stones.

I continue on my way, contemplating the diversity of the human mind. I recall the advice of Paul Cézanne, how he urged young painters to view nature as a profusion of cones, rectangles, circles, and squares. That was how he perceived the world, and day after day, in still life and landscape, he painted what he saw. "Not since Moses has anyone looked at a mountain so greatly," the poet Rainer Maria Rilke wrote upon viewing a memorial exhibition of his work.

Geometric shapes impressed the Greek mathematician Pythagoras in a different way. When he observed a right triangle, he was moved not to paint but to calculate, which is an art of a different kind. He determined that the square of the hypotenuse equals the sum of the squares of the other two sides. When I studied geometry ages ago, I accepted its theorems as given truths handed down by an irrefutable god. But now I ask myself what manner of man looks at a triangle, filters it through his brain, and formulates an equation that reveals the affinity among its angles and sides?

The mind vibrates like the strings of a harp in accord with what it perceives. One man beholds nature and produces a painting, another an equation, another a cluster of statues along the shore. Each discovers his own métier, which is a way of saying he expresses what he thinks and feels in his own distinctive way. The style is personal and particular; it does not arise from a conscious decision, but flows as a river flows out of hidden springs.

The graceful performers of my lifetime rise in memory: Fred Astaire in dance, Ella Fitzgerald in song, Benny Goodman on the clarinet, Joe DiMaggio in center field. I believe the talent was present in them, as it is in everyone, from birth, from before birth, and they felt its tidal pull guiding them, directing them, from an early age. Astaire did not choose the dance; the dance chose him. He had no choice but to tap his feet or die.

There is a telling piece of dialogue between Astaire and Ginger Rogers in the classic film *Top Hat*:

> FRED: You see every once in a while I suddenly find myself . . . dancing.
>
> GINGER: Oh, I suppose it's some kind of affliction.
>
> FRED: Yes, yes . . . it's an affliction. . . . I think I feel an attack coming on.

Hands, feet, head, and body—they all appear to be flying in different directions, and yet there is symmetry, fluency, abandon in every step, lightness and verve in every turn, and no wasted movement anywhere. The style is not contrived, not imposed; it comes from the brio of the dancer himself, and it is distinctly his own.

There is no cure for an "affliction" of this nature; one must give in to it, cultivate it through constant practice, endless rehearsal, until the gift that comes from a power beyond ourselves is perfectly honed.

The popular presumption is that it is easy for talented people to do what comes naturally. Fred, Ella, Benny, Joe—everything they did appeared unrestrained, as if there were never a time when they skipped a beat, missed a note, or dropped a long fly ball. Even the sculptor down the beach wants me to believe that he picks up rocks and stacks them in an abstract, mindless way. But I wonder what sacrifices he made, what self-doubts he overcame, to attain the clarity of vision that inspires his forms.

Vincent van Gogh addressed the struggle of the artist, the struggle of everyman, in a letter to his brother, Theo:

> And great things are not something accidental, but must certainly be willed. What is drawing? How does one learn it? It is working through an invisible iron wall that stands between what one feels and what one can do.

If I did not know it before, I know it now: Throughout my adult life I, too, have been trying to break through an invisible iron wall. I have come closer to achieving that goal here on the sands of Miramar than anyplace I have ever dwelled before. The journey has not been easy; I still have a distance to travel before I fully arrive. But I am on my way toward the center of myself, doing my best to strip away layers of sham and pretense as I go along.

I believe we experience the pulse of our talent coursing through our bodies when we are young. The passion drives us on. We know intuitively who we are and where we must go, in the same way birds know the migratory routes they must follow north in spring and south in fall. But as we mature, we adopt patterns of behavior that stand between ourselves and what we feel.

When I was a boy, I wrote as I wanted to write, never striving for cleverness, for I was too young to know what cleverness was. The words sprang out of my raw emotion, and the children who were my classmates and friends laughed and cried when the teacher asked me to read aloud. But when I became a man, I began to write for the approval and applause of others, who I thought controlled my destiny. It wasn't until I went back to my childhood, to writing the way I wanted to write, thinking the way I wanted to think, feeling the way I wanted to feel, that the words rose easily again.

The creation of an authentic work of art, the creation of an authentic life—they are one and the same. Neither can be accomplished as long as affectation obstructs the way. The life that lives behind a mask, that calls attention to itself, is doomed to fail.

I once knew a man who died of the mask he wore. For a long time I thought we were close friends. When I was told that he had killed himself, I sank to my knees, as if I had been struck a mortal blow from behind. I couldn't understand how someone who possessed so much charm, so much confidence, so much common sense, could take his own life.

I gave the eulogy at his funeral, and I mourned—for him and for me. I realized that this man who I had thought was my friend was really a stranger. All I ever saw, all I ever knew, was the wit and conviviality that covered up the agony he bore.

And Richard Cory, one calm summer night,
Went home and put a bullet through his head.

When I first came upon those lines by Edwin Arlington Robinson, I was a sophomore in high school and I didn't know what they meant. How could someone like Richard Cory, who "fluttered pulses when he said Good-morning," who "was rich—yes richer than a king," who "was admirably schooled in every grace," go home one night and put a bullet through his head?

But the poet knew what I didn't know—couldn't know—as a youth. He knew that Richard Cory isn't an anomaly; he is a familiar figure who strolls the streets of his town, pausing here and there to chat with people he knows. He is always cordial, always neatly attired. But what he presents is not himself but a counterfeit picture of himself, a carefully composed disguise to impress those he encounters along the way. And so his life is not a real life; it's a masquerade.

The world is filled with Richard Corys. They are dying, just as my friend was dying without my knowing it. They are dying slowly, dying inevitably, because, whether they admit it or not, they despise the person they pretend to be and lack the courage to become the person they are.

I do not know what plagued my friend, and now I never will. Perhaps he was beset by a profound moral dilemma that he dared not disclose. Gay men and women talk about "coming out of the closet," as if they are the only ones too ashamed to show their true selves. But since the suicide of my friend I have come to believe that many of us would sooner die than remove our masks and stand barefaced before the world.

An elderly couple, walking arm in arm, approach me on the beach. The woman has thick lips, a bulging nose, a large wart on her cheek. The man is bald; he has thick black eyebrows and a heavy double chin. They are barefoot, strolling slowly, absorbed in their conversation, but as they pass, they turn to me and nod pleasantly, as if, for a moment, to admit me into their company.

It occurs to me that the woman could cover her blemishes with makeup; the man could undergo a face-lift. With the aid of a beautician and plastic surgeon they could present a much different countenance to onlookers and passersby. But if they did, the false face would dictate what they said and how they behaved, and they would lose the genuineness of their smiles, which light the day.

On my desk in my beach house, I have an array of postcard portraits. The faces are so flushed with life. One is a study of St. Ambrose by Peter Paul Rubens, the massive head, the crooked nose, the curly beard, the intent eyes. Is this how St. Ambrose looked, or is the portrait the consummation of Rubens's fertile imaginings? St. Ambrose died twelve hundred years before Rubens was born. But in the painting the two men merge: The guileless artist shows us the guileless saint.

There are other portraits in my personal gallery. A flirtatious young girl raising her veil by Bartolomé Esteban Murillo. A serene young woman by Edgar Degas. A despondent man by Paul Cézanne. A blithesome butterfly girl by Winslow Homer. Whenever I look at them, I become convinced that the hope of the world lies not with churchmen, statesmen, or politicians, but with men and women like these who have banished pretense from their lives.

One by one they go forth, affecting by their

presence the way we think and act. *They are the light of the world. Like a city set on a hill, they can not be hid.*

Occupied with these thoughts, I barely notice the passage of time. Before I realize it, I am at the post office, where I stop twice a week to pick up my mail. My box is low; I have to stoop to remove the contents. As I rise, I turn and confront a scraggly-haired woman in a rumpled dress who is looking up at me with a foolish grin.

I have seen her before, riding her rickety bike down the dirt road that leads to the beach, moving from one trash can to the next, searching for empty bottles and cans and scraps of food.

"I know who you are!" she says in a loud voice. "You're the beachcomber of Miramar!"

It's noon; the post office is crowded with people buying stamps, posting packages, sorting through their mail. They stop and stare. I want to flee. But the urge passes as quickly as it came.

"The beachcomber of Miramar?" I reply. "Yes, that's exactly who I am."

seventeen

ebb tide

I wake before dawn, pull on clothes, and go down to the edge of the sea. The wind is light, the swells huge, the phosphors sparking like dying embers in the luminescent curl of the waves. I am here alone, as I have been so many nights before. The waning moon floats down the western sky. Under its glimmering light, the deep sea rolls in ceaseless motion toward the shore, grinding rock and soil into grains of sand.

It wasn't easy, this journey to Miramar. But I am here now, having crossed many rivers and many hills. What I desire more than anything else, sitting here on this moonlit beach at this moment, is to feel the slow, steady march of my existence, the continuum of my days.

I have lived a long life already; I am astounded how far back my memories go, how much the years contain. . . .

I am thirteen and I am strolling along a spit of

sand where the Atlantic Ocean meets the Great South Bay. The tide is ebbing, as it is now; I am at the tender age of discovery, when every speckled shell conveys its own surprise. Razor clams, cherrystones, periwinkles, horseshoe crabs—they are strewn across the beach, and I have no way of knowing what I might stumble on as I wade through the shoals.

I see an airhole and carefully dig around it with the cup of my hand until I uncover a delicate soft-shell clam. I find twenty, fifty, a hundred, and I put them in saltwater pools exactly like the ones that surround me now. I let them wash for an hour. When I lift them out, they are a delicacy, cleansed of sand, ready for the steam pot.

In recalling that boy, I recall my former self, the child I pushed so far down into the base of my being when I became a man that I forgot he was there. Now, all these years later, I realize how much I miss him, how much I want him back again.

I glance anxiously over the crest of the waves. The images of my past appear before me, the people I have known, the places I have been, the sorrow of what once was and can never be again. My parents mated, then died before they were old enough to see me grown. I married; my wife and I raised children of our own before our marriage failed and we parted. I pursued a career that frustrated me; I quit and went off in a different direction, regretting the years I had wasted, the energy I had spent.

Why was I made to endure such loss so young? Why did I choose a woman so wrong for me? Why did I let finances determine the course of my career? Confused, I made my pilgrimage to Miramar, and now, at long last, I believe I understand.

Loss, waste, regret, sorrow, pain—these are the judgments of a man, not the concerns of a child. When I wandered the beach as a youth, I did not pass sentence on every step I took, every turn I made, every treasure I found. I accepted the events of my life, embraced them for what they were, what they are. I welcomed the unexpected, held fast to the unknown, moved in sympathy with the wind and rain. Only after I was grown did I try to give a name—life, death, good, evil, joy, sorrow—to the occurrences that mark my journey through this world.

The events of my life are like the rolling of the waves, the changing of the tide, the shifting of the wind—they contain no judgment. My parents' death was not a tragedy, my marriage not a mistake, my career not a miscalculation. They were the course of my days, the pattern of my years, the flow of the life that was given to me, and the way I lived it.

I watch the dawn come slowly over the dunes.

Offshore a string of brown pelicans soars so close to the water, their wings seem to touch the sea. They climb and circle; from the beach they look like miniature pterodactyls diving for prey. I have at times seen so many of them gathered overhead, crisscrossing and dropping through the leaden sky, that they appear as inseparable as driving rain.

More than a dozen are fishing; gulls trail every one. I single out one pelican and follow his flight; I watch him hover and plunge, twisting his body, tucking back his wings an instant before he strikes the sea. As soon as he surfaces, two gulls attack; they sit on his head and peck at his bill, trying to force him to cough up his catch.

The pelican raises his pouch, drains the water, swallows his fish, and takes off again, circling the sky with rhythmic wing beats, pursued by gulls. He knows they will be following him wherever he flies, taunting him whenever he dives, but he is undeterred. He soars, aware only of what he was meant to do. His purpose is to dive for anchovies; mine to comb the sand.

A jogger comes at me through the morning mist; I can tell by his gait he's a bulldog of a man. As he nears, I see his neck is as thick as his thighs, which churn like pistons as he plows through the heavy sand. Ankle-deep, he sloshes by; twenty minutes later I hear him bearing down on me from behind and he passes me a second time. I chase after him; I want to find out if I can match his pace, but after a hundred yards I see a tanker far out to sea. I stop and watch it make its passage across the horizon, looking as if it might at any moment slip sideways over the rim of the world.

When I was a young man, I was consumed by practical considerations. I measured my progress by external matters: the balance in my bank account, the kind of house I lived in, my advancement on the job. I divided my life into compartments, commuting daily between work and play. I was striving, constantly striving, without even knowing what I was striving for.

Now I am weary of struggling; I do not want to struggle anymore. I do not want to please; I do not need the trappings of money, power, or success. I do not seek a trophy on my wall or a corner office with a potted plant. I do not desire a house that others envy every time they drive by. All I want is a life that is my own.

Somewhere within my being lies an inviolate place, born of the sun, moving toward the sun all the time. It has been there all along, the sum of all I am and all I aspire to be, that aspect of my nature I call my soul. Silently this force within me has gathered its own momentum and led me here to Miramar.

My life, from its beginning to this very moment, has been a grand migration. Slowly, instinctively,

I have been tending toward this time and place where I could shed the arbitrary boundaries of existence laid down by practical people and live my life.

The tide is out, all the way out, and the long, sloping flat, where waves washed a few hours earlier, is now exposed. I head back to my beach house, my bare feet sinking into the soft, wet sand. The freshening sea wind is in my face; the sun, halfway up the morning sky, is on my back. I think of pancakes. I quicken my pace; the craving increases with every step. I can go inside, mix the batter, and heat the griddle. I climb the steps to my beach house's deck. Even before I open the door, I can taste the syrup.